THE JAMES W. RICHARDS LECTURES IN HISTORY

THE UNIVERSITY OF VIRGINIA

☆ ☆ ☆

MAJORITY RULE AND MINORITY RIGHTS

TO

FELIX FRANKFURTER

WHOSE OPINIONS CONFESS
AN UNDISMAYED FAITH
IN DEMOCRACY

MAJORITY RULE

and Minority Rights

By HENRY STEELE COMMAGER

OXFORD UNIVERSITY PRESS
LONDON NEW YORK TORONTO
1943

First Printing, September, 1943
Second Printing, February, 1944

A WARTIME BOOK

THIS COMPLETE EDITION IS PRODUCED IN FULL COMPLIANCE WITH THE GOVERNMENT'S REGULATIONS FOR CONSERVING PAPER AND OTHER ESSENTIAL MATERIALS.

PRINTED IN THE UNITED STATES OF AMERICA

☆ ☆

CONTENTS

☆ ☆

I

Majority Rule and Minority Rights

'A GRAVE RESPONSIBILITY confronts this Court,' said Mr. Justice Frankfurter in presenting the majority opinion in the Gobities case, 'whenever in the course of litigation it must reconcile the conflicting claims of liberty and authority.' [1] That opinion held that 'except where the transgression of constitutional liberty is too plain for argument, personal freedom is best maintained—as long as the remedial channels of the democratic process remain open and unobstructed—where it is ingrained in a people's habits and not enforced against popular policy by the coercion of adjudicated law,' and sustained the constitutionality of the flag-salute requirement by the Minersville School District. Perhaps the most remarkable thing about this opinion was that it was so widely, I might say all but universally, misunderstood.[2] Liberals—or those who regarded themselves as such—almost to a man denounced the opinion as illiberal and celebrated the dissenting opinion written by the Chief Justice. The apparent inability of most Americans today to understand the logic and the implications of Mr. Justice Frankfurter's opinion suggests the desirability, indeed the imperative necessity, of a reconsideration of the basic problem it presents: the problem of majority rule *versus* limited government.

This is, to be sure, a very old problem—as old as government itself: it is a universal problem, pressing everywhere for solution. But it is not too much to assert that it is a problem that can best be understood in connection with American experience. For it was in America that the doctrine of majority rule was first successfully asserted and effectuated; it was in America that the principle of limited government was first institutionalized and that machinery for maintaining it was first fashioned.

These statements may require some elaboration. What we have here are two fundamental—perhaps the two most fundamental—principles of American politics: the principle that men make government, and the principle that there are limits to the authority of government. The philosophical origins of the first principle may be found in the natural-rights philosophy of the seventeenth century—in the notion that all rights inhered originally in men and that men, living in a state of nature, came together for mutual self-protection and set up government, and that the governments thus instituted derive all their just powers from the consent of the governed. However sound this may be as a description of an historical process—and Jefferson for one did not question its soundness—it was indubitably a correct description of what had happened in the New World from the time of the Mayflower Compact on to the organization of government along the banks of the Holston and the Watauga and the Tennessee, and of what was to happen, again and again, along the frontier from the Blue Ridge to the Willamette.[3]

The second great basic principle—that governments are limited, that there are things no government may do, rights no government may impair, powers no government may exercise—traces its philosophical origins deep into the past but again derives authority from American experience with Parliamentary and royal pretensions. It held, simply enough, that as government was instituted to secure certain rights, its jurisdiction was strictly limited to the fields assigned to it, and that if it overstepped the bounds of its jurisdiction its acts were not law. In the great words of Samuel Adams, addressed to Shelburne and Rockingham and Camden, 'in all free states the constitution is fixed; it is from thence that the legislative derives its authority; therefore it cannot change the constitution without destroying its own foundations.'[4]

But Americans did more than espouse and formulate these political principles. The great achievement of the men of the Revolutionary era was that, in the words of old John Adams, 'they realized the doctrines of the wisest writers.' They institutionalized their principles. They fashioned a mechanism for putting into effect the idea that men make government. This was, needless to say, the institution of the constitutional convention that provided a legal and perfectly peaceful method of altering or abolishing governments and creating new ones. It is no exaggeration to say that this institution of the constitutional convention was—with the possible exception of the federal system—the greatest political invention to come out of the New World.[5]

And that same generation, more conscious of the dangers than of the potentialities of government, more concerned with protection against governmental tyranny than with the promotion of majority welfare, devised cunning mechanisms for putting limitations upon government. When we contemplate the ingenuity of the Fathers in setting up their system of checks and balances we are deeply impressed, almost dismayed. That the limits of governmental authority might not be misunderstood, that authority was described—for the first time—in written constitutions, and to these constitutions were added bills of rights. But this was merely elementary. There were, in addition, the checks and balances of the federal system, of the tripartite division of powers, of the bicameral legislatures, of frequent elections, and of impeachment. And atop all this there developed—I would not say there was established—the practice of judicial review.

But in their laudable zeal to give reality to John Dickinson's description of a free people—'Not those over whom government is reasonably and equitably exercised, but those who live under a government so constitutionally checked and controuled, that proper provision is made against its being otherwise exercised'—the framers of our constitutions confused, it would seem, jurisdiction with power, and the confusion has persisted down to our own day. They failed properly to distinguish between the authority government should have, and the manner in which government might exercise that authority which it did have. They set up limits on the jurisdiction of government, enumerating things no government could do; and this was eminently proper and in harmony with the philosophy of the Revolutionary era. But they went farther. So fearful were they of governmental tyranny that even where they granted to government certain necessary powers they put obstacles in the way of the effective exercise of those powers. They set up not only boundaries to government but impediments in government. Thus they not only made it difficult for government to invade fields denied to it, but they made it difficult for government to operate at all. They created a system where deadlock would be the normal character of the American government—a situation from which political parties rescued us.[6]

So here we have two institutions which are—or would appear to be—fundamentally contradictory. We have first the institutionalization of the principle that men can alter, abolish, and institute governments, can, in short, make government conform to their will. But over against this we have the institutionalization of the principle that governments are limited—that there are things not even a majority may require government to do because they are outside the jurisdiction of any government. If the majority may use government to do its will, is that not an attack upon the inalienable rights of men over against government? if there are limits upon what government may do, is that not a challenge to or even a denial of the principle of majority rule? Here is a paradox not yet resolved in our political philosophy or our constitutional system.

This paradox is presented in most familiar form in Jefferson's First Inaugural Address: 'All, too, will bear in mind this sacred principle, that though the will of the majority is in all cases to prevail, that will to be rightful must be reasonable; that the minority possess their equal rights which equal law must protect, and to violate would be oppression.' And throughout our history runs this theme of majority will and minority rights. Jefferson, as we shall see, emphasized majority will, and so did Jefferson's successors, Jackson and Lincoln—Jackson, who brushed aside judicial interposition,[7] Lincoln, who reminded us that

> A majority . . . is the only true sovereign of a free people. Whoever rejects it does, of necessity, fly into anarchy or to despotism. Unanimity is impossible; the rule of a minority, as a permanent arrangement, is wholly inadmissable; so that, rejecting the majority principle, anarchy or despotism in some form is all that is left.[8]

But the emphasis since the Civil War has been increasingly on minority rights—an emphasis so marked, between Reconstruction and the New Deal, that it is no great exaggeration to say that tenderness for the minority became the distinguishing characteristic of the American constitutional system.

Underlying this distinction are, of course, the assumptions that majority will and minority rights are antithetical, that majority rule constantly threatens minority rights, and that the principal function of our constitutional system is to protect minority rights against infringement.

So plausible are these assumptions that there has developed, in course of time, the theory of the 'tyranny of the majority'—a theory which derived much support abroad as well as here from the misleading observations of Tocqueville. Tocqueville, who leaned heavily for material and authority on that pillar of conservatism, Joseph Story,[9] confessed that 'the very essence of democratic government consists in the absolute sovereignty of the majority,' and concluded from this that the prospects for American democracy were bleak indeed.[10] His analysis of the consequences that flow from the tyranny of the majority has given comfort, ever since, to those who fear democracy. So persuasive is this theory of the tyranny of the majority that many Americans have come to believe that our constitutional system is not, in fact, based upon the principle of majority rule. And they have found support and consolation in the curious notion that ours is a 'republican' form of government, and that a republic is the very opposite of a democracy.

The fear of the tyranny of the majority has haunted many of the most distinguished and respectable American statesmen and jurists since the days of the founding of the Republic; it persists today, after a century and a half of experience. It was first formulated, in elaborate and coherent fashion, by John Adams in his famous *Defense of the Constitutions of Government of the United States of America* (1786). The people, Adams urges, are not to be trusted, nor are their representatives, without an adequate system of checks and balances:

If it is meant by the people . . . a representative assembly, . . . they are not the best keepers of the people's liberties or their own, if you give them all the power, legislative, executive and judicial. They would invade the liberties of the people, at least the majority of them would invade the liberties of the minority, sooner and oftener than any absolute monarch.

Anticipating the arguments to be used again and again in the next century, Adams appealed to the experience of the past and conjured up hypothetical dangers in the future:

The experience of all ages has proved, that they [the people] constantly give away their liberties into the hands of grandees, or kings, idols of their own creation. The management of the executive and judicial powers together always corrupts them, and throws the whole power into the hands of the most profligate and abandoned among them.

And if the majority were to control all branches of the government:

Debts would be abolished first; taxes laid heavy on the rich, and not at all on the others; and at last a downright equal division of everything be demanded and voted. The idle, the vicious, the intemperate, would rush into the utmost extravagance of debauchery, sell and spend all their share, and then demand a new division of those who purchased from them. The moment the idea is admitted into society, that property is not as sacred as the laws of God, and that there is not a force of law and public justice to protect it, anarchy and tyranny commence.[11]

That other great apostle of conservatism, Alexander Hamilton, approached the subject of majority rule in far more circumspect fashion.

It was a thing hardly to be expected [he wrote in No. 26 of the *Federalist*] that in a popular revolution the minds of men should stop at that happy mean which marks the salutary boundary between POWER and PRIVILEGE, and combines the energy of government with the security of private rights. A failure in this delicate and important point is the great source of the inconveniences we experience, and if we are not cautious to avoid a repetition of the error, in our future attempts to rectify and ameliorate our system, we may travel from one chimerical project to another . . .

And, in No. 51, he warned his countrymen that

It is of great importance in a republic not only to guard the society against the oppression of its rulers, but to guard one part of the society against the injustice of the other part. Different interests necessarily exist in different classes of citizens. If a majority be united by a common interest, the rights of the minority will be insecure . . . Justice is the end of government. It is the end of civil society . . . In a society under the forms of which the stronger faction can readily unite and oppress the weaker, anarchy may as truly be said to reign as in a state of nature where the weaker individual is not secured against the violence of the stronger.

In the privacy of the Federal Convention Hamilton has been even more candid. 'The voice of the people,' he said in his famous diatribe against the Virginia and New Jersey plans,

has been said to be the voice of God; and however generally this maxim has been quoted and believed, it is not true to fact. The people are turbulent and changing, they seldom judge or determine right. Give therefore to the [rich] a distinct, permanent share in the government. They will check the unsteadiness of the second . . . Can a democratic Assembly, who annually revolve in the mass of the people, be supposed steadily to pursue the public good? Nothing but a permanent body can check the imprudence of democracy. Their turbulent and uncontrolling disposition requires checks.[12]

Later publicists were to ring the changes on this theme again and again: the majority would surrender its power to a despot—or a boss—; it would plunder the rich; it would oppress minorities; it would destroy the liberties of men. Thus doughty old Chancellor Kent, resisting the proposal for broadening the suffrage in New York State:

By the report before us we propose to annihilate, at one stroke, all those property distinctions and to bow before the idol of universal suffrage. That extreme democratic principle, when applied to the legislative and executive departments of government, has been regarded with terror, by the wise men of every age, because in every European republic, ancient and modern, in which it has been tried, it has terminated disastrously, and been productive of corruption, injustice, violence, and tyranny. And dare we flatter ourselves that we are a peculiar people, who can run the career of history, exempted from the passions which have disturbed and corrupted the rest of mankind? [13]

So, too, the learned Justice Story threw the great weight of his prestige against the proposal that a majority had a right to alter their form of government.[14] So Calhoun dedicated his splendid talents to the formulation of an ingenious system designed to arrest the exercise of the tyranny of the majority against the peculiar institution,[15] and his great opponent, Daniel Webster, was no less zealous to protect the inherited rights of well-entrenched minorities against majority interference.[16] By mid-century the anti-majority theory was fully formulated, and it is pertinent to recall why and by whom it was formulated. It was formulated in defense of property interests allegedly threatened by majority greed by those who put property rights above human rights. It was formulated by those who already had political privileges and were determined that the common man should not share them. It was formulated in defense of slavery in the just fear that slavery and majority rule were ultimately incompatible. It was formulated, in short, by those who proved themselves completely out of harmony with the fundamental tendencies of American society and who have been rejected by the American people.

The latter-day representatives of the minority-rights doctrine—a motley group—have been neither as distinguished nor as plausible as their predecessors. In Theodore Woolsey, William Graham Sumner, John W. Burgess, Henry Cabot Lodge, James M. Beck, Henry L. Mencken, Ralph Adams Cram, Walter Lippmann, Dorothy Thompson, and Isabel Patterson, in the learned jurists Cooley and Field and Brewer and Sutherland and McReynolds, the argument is less assured, the logic less coherent, the shrill note more frequent. And the contemporary presentation is almost completely lacking in the dignity and in the muscular intellectual toughness that characterized the argument of Adams and Calhoun and Webster. For our edification it is conveniently epitomized and assembled in the six volumes of the *Hearings of the Senate Judiciary Committee* on the court reform bill of 1937—where we may consult it, though whether either with pleasure or with profit is a matter of opinion.[17]

Confronted by these different interpretations of the American constitutional system, of democracy and of republicanism, we may turn with some confidence to Thomas Jefferson. On these questions he is, indubitably, our leading authority. He helped to create and to establish the new political systems in America, and he furnished them with a good part of their political philosophy. He never wrote a formal treatise on the subject (as did his old friend John Adams), but in his public papers and his private letters we can find the most comprehensive and consistent statement of the nature of American democracy that has come down to us from the generation of the founders.

And it must be observed, first, that Jefferson was by no means unaware of the dangers inherent in majority rule. He had had experience with recalcitrant assemblies in Virginia; he had watched, on the whole with approval, but not without misgivings, the course of rule by succeeding—and ever more radical—assemblies in France; he had rallied the forces of liberalism against legislative tyranny as represented in the Alien and Sedition Acts. His proposed constitution for Virginia provided a complicated system of checks and balances; [18] his *Notes on Virginia* counted it 'precisely the definition of despotic government' that 'all powers of government, legislative, executive, and judiciary, result to the legislative body.' [19] Writing to his friend James Madison, in 1789, he had counselled against the 'tyranny of legislatures' as 'the most formidable dread,' [20] and the following year he had reaffirmed, to Noah Webster, his conviction that there were rights beyond the jurisdiction of 'ordinary' government.[21] The Kentucky Resolutions, which he drafted, contained an eloquent expression of the doctrine that the majority of the national legislature might not violate the terms of the compact the states had made, and the first annual message to the Congress—in its original form—repudiated legislative omnipotence where personal liberties were concerned.

Yet none of these things implies distrust of majority rule, for majority rule is neither anarchy nor absolutism, but government within self-imposed restraints. And we search in vain through the voluminous writings of Jefferson for any expression of distrust of the virtue or the wisdom of the people. What we do find, on the contrary, from the beginning to the end of Jefferson's career, is an unterrified and unflinching faith in majority rule.

'I am not among those who fear the people,' he wrote to Kercheval in 1816; 'they and not the rich, are our dependence for continued freedom.' [22] It was the reiteration of an argument that the author of the Declaration of Independence found it necessary to make with increasing frequency. Back in 1787 he had had to reassure many of his friends, who were stampeded by the Shays' rebellion into a reaction against democracy. Writing to Madison from Paris he pointed out the true solution of the problem which that uprising presented:

> Educate and inform the whole mass of the people. Enable them to see that it is their interest to preserve peace and order, and they will preserve them. And it requires no very high degree of education to convince them of this. They are the only sure reliance for the preservation of our liberty.

After all, it is my principle that the will of the majority should prevail.[23]

And to another Virginia friend, Colonel Carrington, went the same reassurance:

The tumults in America I expected would have produced in Europe an unfavorable opinion of our political state. But it has not. On the contrary, the small effect of these tumults seems to have given more confidence in the firmness of our governments. The interposition of the people themselves on the side of government has had a great effect on the opinion here. I am persuaded myself that the good sense of the people will always be found to be the best army. They may be led astray for a moment, but will soon correct themselves. The people are the only censors of their governors; and even their errors will tend to keep these to the true principles of their institution.[24]

That the people, if led astray, would 'soon correct themselves' was a fixed conviction and one which, *mirabile dictu*, found confirmation in their tenacious support of his own administration. Thus to John Tyler in 1804:

No experiment can be more interesting than that we are now trying, and which we trust will end in establishing the fact that man may be governed by reason and truth . . . The firmness with which the people have withstood the late abuses of the press, the discernment that they have manifested between truth and falsehood, show that they may safely be trusted to hear everything true and false, and to form correct judgment between them . . .[25]

This was the consistent note—that the people may—and must—be trusted. 'No government can continue good,' he assured John Adams, 'but under the control of the people'; [26] and again, to that doughty opponent of judicial pretensions, Spencer Roane, 'Independence can be trusted nowhere but with the people in the mass. They are inherently independent of all but the moral law.' [27] 'I know of no safe depository of the ultimate powers of the society,' he told William Jarvis, 'but the people themselves; and if we think them not enlightened enough to exercise their control with a wholesome discretion, the remedy is not to take it from them, but to inform their discretion by education.' [28] And recalling Hume's argument that 'all history and experience' confounded the notion that 'the people are the origin of all just power,' Jefferson burst out with uncharacteristic violence: 'And where else will this degenerate son of science, this traitor to his fellow men, find the origin of just powers, if not in the majority of the society? Will it be in the minority? Or in an individual of that minority?' [29] And we hear an echo of that question which the First Inaugural submits to the contemporary world: 'Sometimes it is said that man can not be trusted with the government of himself. Can he, then, be trusted with the government of others? Or have we found angels in the forms of kings to govern him? Let history answer this question.' For himself, Jefferson knew the answer. His devotion to the people was not that of the benevolent despot, the party boss, or the dictator, but of the good citizen, and his whole career is a monument to the sincerity of his confession to Du Pont de Nemours.

We both love the people, he said, 'but you love them as infants, whom you are afraid to trust without nurses; and I as adults whom I freely leave to self-government.' [30]

To all of this many of Jefferson's contemporaries could have subscribed without reservation: he, assuredly, had no monopoly on faith in popular government. 'We of the United States,' as he explained simply, 'are constitutionally and conscientiously democrats.' [31] But in one respect Jefferson went farther than most of his contemporaries, went so far, indeed, that his argument sounds bizarre and almost alien to our ears. That was his advocacy of what we may call the doctrine of the continuing majority. It was easy enough for most Americans to subscribe to the compact theory of government—the compact made, of course, by the original majority—just as it is easy for us to subscribe, now, to the doctrine that we are, all of us, bound by the compact made at Philadelphia in 1787 and ratified by the majority of that time. And just as we have invested that Constitution with sacrosanctity,[32] so—in England, in France, in America of the eighteenth century—there was a tendency to regard the original compact, the product of the Golden Age of the past, with reverence and to invest it with a peculiar sanctity. Such an attitude was foreign to Jefferson. His conviction, however, that each new majority must write its own fundamental law has sometimes been regarded as merely an amusing exaggeration, a whimsey to be indulged along with the whimsey that a little rebellion, now and then, is an excellent thing. But there can be no doubt of Jefferson's sincerity in the matter, nor of his persuasion that the issue was one of fundamental importance.

This problem is more fundamental, and more complex, than might appear at first glance—this problem of the original *versus* the continuing majority. All of us seem to agree that we are bound by the original majority—by the majority of 1787, or that which decreed our state constitutions. But what if the will of the present majority conflicts with that of the original majority? Is majority will valid only for some past generation? The easy answer is that the present majority can, if it chooses, change the original compact by constitutional amendment or by substituting an entirely new constitution. But it takes more than a majority to amend a constitution or to write a new one, and under our present system a determined minority can, if it will, effectively veto any change in the federal document and in most state documents. Not only this, but the courts have pretty consistently held that the current majority may not even interpret the original constitution to accommodate it to felt needs. The whole issue was luridly dramatized in the Dorr Rebellion—now almost forgotten—and in the great case of Luther *v.* Borden—now quite forgotten; the conclusion that emerged from this episode—less than a quarter century after Jefferson's death—was that under our system the original controls the current majority.[33]

Whatever may have been the wisdom or the expediency of that conclusion—and the actual decision in Luther *v.* Borden went on other grounds—it cannot well be maintained that it was in accordance with the philosophy of majority rule; it may be doubted that it was in harmony with the political philosophy of the Fathers; it may even be questioned whether it was sound constitutional law. This is not the place to review the complex and controversial issues involved in the Dorr Rebellion or Luther *v.* Borden, or to reappraise the learned argument of Benjamin Hallett,[34] but it may be suggested that the authorities he cited in defense of the power of the present majority to override earlier majorities are persuasive. One of these, needless to say, was Jefferson. It is curious rather than important that another was Marshall himself.

Jefferson, as we know, entertained no reverence for the constitutional dogmas of the past. His attitude, set forth in the famous letter to Samuel Kercheval, of July 1816, is too familiar to justify quotation in full:

> Let us [not] weakly believe that one generation is not as capable as another of taking care of itself, and of ordering its own affairs. Let us . . . avail ourselves of our reason and experience, to correct the crude essays of our first and unexperienced, although wise, virtuous and well-meaning counsels. And lastly, let us provide in our Constitution for its revision at stated periods. What these periods should be, nature herself indicates . . . Each generation is as independent of the one preceding, as that was of all which had gone before. It has, then, like them, a right to choose for

itself the form of government it believes most promotive of its own happiness . . . and it is for the peace and good of mankind that a solemn opportunity of doing this every nineteen or twenty years should be provided by the Constitution.[35]

This was no fleeting notion, inspired by dissatisfaction with the Virginia constitution and the proposal to call a new constitutional convention, but a settled conviction. Back in France, it would appear, he had discussed this principle with LaFayette and his friends when they were preparing the Declaration of the Rights of Man,[36] and at the same time he had written to Madison that he supposed it 'self-evident'

that the earth belongs in usufruct to the living; that the dead have neither power nor rights over it . . . No society can make a perpetual constitution, or even a perpetual law. The earth belongs always to the living generation; they may manage it, then, and what proceeds from it, as they please, during the usufruct . . . Every constitution, then, and every law, naturally expires at the end of thirty-four years. If it be enforced longer, it is an act of force and not of right.

And he added, with reference to repeals of amendments:

It may be said, that the succeeding generation, exercising, in fact, the power of repeal, this leaves them as free as if the constitution or law had been expressly limited to thirty-four years only. In the first place this objection admits the right, in proposing an equivalent. But the power of repeal is not an equivalent. It might be, indeed, if every form of government were so perfectly contrived that the will of the majority could always be obtained, fairly and without impediment. But this is true of no form . . . A law of limited duration is much more manageable than one which needs a repeal.[37]

Again and again Jefferson returned to this proposition. Thus, to his friend John Eppes, in 1813: 'We may consider each generation as a distinct nation, with a right, by the will of the majority, to bind themselves, but none to bind the succeeding generation, more than the inhabitants of another country.'[38] The controversy over the reorganization of Dartmouth College evoked a letter to Governor Plumer which, when compared with the opinions of Marshall and Story in the Dartmouth College case, suggests strikingly the difference between the doctrines of the original and the continuing majority.

The idea that institutions established for the use of the nation cannot be touched or modified, even to make them answer their end, because of rights gratuitously supposed in those employed to manage them in trust for the public, may perhaps be a salutary provision against the abuses of a monarch, but is most absurd against the nation itself. Yet our lawyers and priests generally inculcate this doctrine, and suppose that preceding generations held the earth more freely than we do; had a right to impose laws on us, unalterable by ourselves, and that we, in like manner, can make laws and impose burdens on future generations, which they will have no right to alter; in fine, that the earth belongs to the dead and not the living.[39]

And in 1825 came perhaps the most succinct statement of these 'self-evident axioms':

That our Creator made the earth for the use of the living and not of the dead; that those who exist not can have no use nor right in it: no authority or power over it; that one generation of men cannot foreclose or burden its use to another, which comes to it in its own right and by the same divine beneficence; that a preceding generation cannot bind a succeeding one by its laws or contracts; these deriving their obligation from the will of the existing majority, and that majority being removed by death, another comes in its place with a will equally free to make its own laws and contracts.[40]

We can dispose more briefly of Jefferson's conception of the nature and meaning of republicanism; were it not for recent and widely publicized misinterpretations [41] of the term, the matter would scarcely merit our attention. The term 'republican'—as a legal rather than a political one—has always presented certain difficulties of precise definition, but it has remained for the undismayed conservatives of our own generation to make the curious discovery that *res publica*—the common thing—is the very antithesis of democracy! [42] Jefferson, who has some claim to have fathered both republicanism and democracy in the United States, was happily unaware of this antithesis, and it is suggestive, at least, that his political party was called successively the Republican, the Republican-Democratic, and the Democratic. On a number of occasions he essayed a definition of the term 'republican.' In 1792 he confided to the *Anas* that he 'took the occasion' to 'lay down the catholic principle of republicanism, to wit, that every people may establish what form of government they please, and change it as they please, the will of the nation being the only thing essential.'[43] Writing to Isaac Tiffany about Aristotle's *Politics* he calls 'a democracy the only pure republic' and urges that 'the republican element of popular control' be 'pushed to the maximum of its practicable exercise.'[44] To his friend Du Pont de Nemours he asserted that 'action by the citizens in person, in affairs within their reach and competence, and in all others by representatives, chosen immediately, and removable by themselves, constitutes the essence of a republic; that all governments are more or less republican in proportion as this principle enters more or less into their composition.'[45] The 'mother principle' of republicanism, he told Kercheval, was 'that governments are republican in proportion as they embody the will of their people, and execute it.'[46] And finally, not to belabor a point sufficiently obvious, we may note Jefferson's attempt clearly to define the term.

> Were I to assign to this term a precise and definite idea [he wrote John Taylor], I would say, purely and simply, it means a government by its citizens in mass, acting directly and personally, according to rules established by the majority; and that every other government is more or less republican in proportion as it has in its composition more or less of this ingredient of the direct action of its citizens.[47]

It is suggestive that most of these observations on the nature of democracy and of republicanism were inspired by the pretensions of the courts to act as the singular interpreters of the Constitution and to interpret the constitutional document (with some aid from the unwritten 'higher law,' useful ever since when the constitutional document appears inadequate) [48] as a limitation on majority will. For it is the courts alone who have formulated a clear-cut and dogmatic answer to the problem we posed at the beginning of our investigation —the problem of majority will and minority rights. That answer has the inestimable advantages of both plausibility and clarity. It has never been more lucidly or succinctly put than by Jefferson's great opponent, Hamilton—from whose argument Marshall draws so freely:

> There is no position which depends on clearer principles than that every act of a delegated authority, contrary to the tenor of the commission under which it is exercised, is void. No legislative act, therefore, contrary to the Constitution can be valid. To deny this would be to affirm that the deputy is greater than his principal . . .
>
> If it be said that the legislative body are themselves the constitutional judges of their own powers, and that the construction they put upon them is conclusive upon the other departments, it may be answered that this cannot be the natural presumption where it is not to be collected from any particular provisions in the Constitution. It is not otherwise to be supposed that the Constitution could intend to enable the representatives of the people to substitute their *will* to that of their constituents. It is far more rational to suppose that the courts were designed to be an intermediate body between the people and the legislature, in order, among other things, to keep the latter within the limits assigned to their authority. The interpretation of the laws

is the proper and peculiar province of the courts. A constitution is, in fact, and must be regarded by the judges, as a fundamental law. It therefore belongs to them to ascertain its meaning, as well as the meaning of any particular act proceeding from the legislative body. If there should happen to be an irreconcilable variance between the two, that which has the superior obligation and validity ought, of course, to be preferred . . .[49]

What Hamilton has reference to—as what Marshall had reference to in his comparable statement in Marbury *v.* Madison[50]—is the review of congressional legislation by federal courts. The same logic would apply to the review of state legislation by state courts. In both of these operations the function of judicial review is to confine majority will to constitutional bounds. The problem of the function of judicial review as a harmonizer of the federal system (though it overlaps the other and larger one) is a distinct one, to be supported or rejected on considerations that have little to do with democracy. It is, needless to say, with the function of judicial review as a check upon democracy that we are concerned.

The argument supporting judicial review, as here set forth by Hamilton, is pat, simple, and by now deeply rooted in our constitutional system and deeply ingrained in our political thinking. It is sometimes forgotten that Jefferson rejected it *in toto*. Let us examine, then, the nature and implications of the judicial solution of the problem of majority will and minority rights and the bases of Jefferson's repudiation of that solution.

☆ ☆

II

Democracy and Judicial Review

TO THE NOTION that no government may overstep the bounds of its jurisdiction, Jefferson would cheerfully have subscribed. No more than Hamilton or Marshall was he willing to yield to a 'palpable infraction of the constitution.' The philosophy behind the great Declaration was that of the compact theory, which held that government was limited, and from this philosophy Jefferson never departed. His influence had been profound in securing the incorporation of a bill of rights into the Constitution [1] and he remained, throughout his career, far more zealous for the maintenance of these rights than did the great Chief Justice—who indeed never showed any particular interest in them.

When confronted by what he held to be legislative violation of these rights—the Alien, Sedition, and Naturalization Acts of 1798—Jefferson reasserted the philosophy of limited government in unmistakable terms:

The several States composing the United States of America, are not united on the principle of unlimited submission to their general government; . . . whensoever the general government assumes undelegated powers, its acts are unauthoritative, void, and of no force . . .

That it would be a dangerous delusion were a confidence in the men of our choice to silence our fears for the safety of our rights; that confidence is everywhere the parent of despotism; free government is founded in jealousy and not in confidence; it is jealousy and not confidence which prescribes limited Constitutions to bind down those whom we are obliged to trust with power: that our Constitution has accordingly fixed the limits to which and no further our confidence may go . . .[2]

And finally:

That the principle . . . that the general government is the exclusive judge of the powers delegated to it, stop not short of *despotism*,—since the discretion of those who administer the government, and not the Constitution, would be the measure of their powers.

But in this emergency he did not turn to the courts—which had for the most part sustained and applied these odious acts[4]—but to the popular branches of the government—the state legislatures. An appeal to the states was the method, a nullification by the states the proper remedy.

The protests by Kentucky and Virginia proved unavailing, but Jefferson was by no means ready to abandon his position. Elected to the presidency he assumed that the executive had an equal right with the other branches of the government to pass upon the constitutionality of legislative acts—even to do this retroactively—and proceeded, in effect, to nullify the unconstitutional acts. As he wrote to Mrs. John Adams:

I discharged every person under punishment or prosecution under the sedition law, because I considered . . . that law to be a nullity as absolute and as palpable as if Congress had ordered us to fall down and worship a golden image; and that it was as much my duty to arrest its execution in every stage as it would have been to have rescued from the fiery furnace those who should have been cast into it for refusing to worship the image. It was accordingly done in every instance, without asking what the offenders had done or against whom they had offended, but whether the pains they were suffering were inflicted under the pretended sedition law.[5]

Writing to Gideon Granger some years later that he had directed 'nolle prosequis in all the prosecutions which had been instituted under' the sedition law, he added the illuminating phrase: 'as far as the public sentiment can be inferred from the occurrences of the day, we may say that this opinion had the sanction of the nation.'[6]

And with this we come to the heart of the problem of judicial review—to the problem never satisfactorily answered, scarcely even asked, by those who accept and defend it. Granted that under our system of government the judiciary is independent and that it is bound by the Constitution—as it understands that document—are not the other departments equally independent, and are they not similarly bound by their own understanding of the document? If the judiciary may re-examine the acts of the legislative and executive departments, why may not these equally re-examine the acts of the judiciary? Is there, in short, to be a double standard of departmental independence? a double standard of constitutional judgment?

Jefferson, clearly, thought not. Each department was competent to judge for itself the meaning of the Constitution. For his first annual message to the Congress he prepared a formal statement of this position—and then omitted it!

Our country has thought proper to distribute the powers of its government among three equal and independent authorities constituting each a check upon one or both of the others in all attempts to impair its constitution. To make each an effectual check it must have a right in cases which arise within the line of its proper function, where equally with the others, it acts in the last resort and without appeal, to decide on the validity of an act according to its own judgment and uncontrolled by the opinions of any other departments . . . On my accession to the administration, reclamations against the sedition act were laid before me by individual citizens claiming the protection of the Constitution against the sedition act. Called on by the position in which the nation had placed me to exercise in their behalf my free and independent judgment, I took that act into consideration, compared it with the Constitution, viewed it under every respect of which I thought it susceptible, and gave it all the attention which the magnitude of the case demanded. On mature deliberation, in the presence of the nation and under the solemn oath which binds me to them,

> and to my duty, I do declare that I hold that act to be in palpable and unqualified contradiction to the Constitution.[7]

This was no mere political whimsey, induced by irritation over judicial acquiescence in the Alien and Sedition Acts. In the year of independence, Jefferson had written his mentor, Judge Wythe, that 'the judicial power ought to be distinct from both the legislative and executive and independent upon them, so that it may be a check upon both, as both should be checks upon that.'[8] In 1804 he pointed out to Abigail Adams that 'nothing in the Constitution has given them [the judges] to decide for the Executive, more than to the Executive to decide for them.' The Constitution 'meant that its co-ordinate branches should be checks upon each other.'[9] The Burr trial confirmed Jefferson in his mistrust of the judicial branch, as did, even more emphatically, that great series of decisions from Martin *v.* Hunter's Lessee to Gibbons *v.* Ogden. By 1815 he held the view that each department was equal and independent in the interpretation of the Constitution to be a conservative one, and was proposing 'another opinion entertained by some men of such judgment and information as to lessen my confidence in my own'—namely, that 'the legislature alone is the exclusive expounder of the sense of the Constitution, in every part of it whatever.'[10]

And as the spectacle of 'judicial despotism' unfolded before him, this opinion seemed increasingly persuasive. In a democracy, he urged, there is really more justification for legislative or executive than for judicial determination of the law, for the decision of the political branches is subject to popular referendum, that of the judicial is not. There had been an interesting anticipation of this argument in Jefferson's attitude toward the Louisiana purchase. That act was, he felt, unconstitutional, and it bothered Jefferson that he should connive at an infraction of the Constitution, even in so good a cause. He had resort then to the saving grace of popular absolution. The treaty must be ratified by both Houses, and

> I suppose they must then appeal to *the nation* for an additional article to the Constitution approving and confirming an act which the nation had not previously authorized. The Constitution has made no provision for our holding foreign territory, still less for incorporating foreign nations into our Union. The executive in seizing the fugitive occurrence which so much advances the good of their country, have done an act beyond the Constitution. The Legislature in casting behind them metaphysical subtleties, and risking themselves like faithful servants, must ratify and pay for it, and throw themselves on their country for doing for them unauthorized, what we know they would have done for themselves had they been in a situation to do it.[11]

But, he concluded almost smugly, 'we shall not be disavowed by the nation, and their act of indemnity will confirm and not weaken the Constitution.'

So though the popular branches might err in their construction of the Constitution there was no need for alarm: the people could be trusted to set them right.

It was the immunity of the judicial branch from popular correction that constituted the real danger. 'It should be remembered as an axiom of eternal truth in politics that whatever power in any government is independent is absolute,' [12] Jefferson warned; and again, 'we have made [judges] independent of the nation itself. They are irremovable, but by their own body, for any depravity of conduct, and even by their own body for the imbecilities of dotage.' [13] And so he arrived at the bold conclusion that the independence of the judiciary was itself a threat to democracy. 'Our judges are effectually independent of the nation,' he confided to his Autobiography:

> But this ought not to be. I would not, indeed, make them dependent on the Executive authority, as they formerly were in England; but I deem it indispensable to the continuance of this government, that they should be submitted to some practical and impartial control . . . I do not charge the Judges with wilful and ill-intentioned error, but honest error must be arrested, where its toleration leads to public ruin. As for the safety of society we must commit honest maniacs to Bedlam, so judges should be withdrawn from the bench, whose erroneous biases are leading us to dissolution.[14]

And proposing specifically that judges be kept on probation by making appointments renewable every four or six years, he concluded that judicial 'independence of the will of the nation, is a solecism, at least in a republican government.' [15]

It is illuminating that Jefferson was prepared to maintain this attitude even with respect to education. Drafting his plans for the teaching of law at his beloved University, he submitted that though in all other subjects the professors must have complete freedom in teaching and in the choice of textbooks, such independence could not be extended to the teaching of law. 'In most public seminaries,' he wrote his co-worker Cabell,

> text-books are prescribed in each of the several schools, as the *norma docendi* in that school; . . . I should not propose this generally in our University, because I believe none of us are so much at the heights of science in the several branches, as to undertake this; and therefore it will be better left to the professors until occasion of interference shall be given. But there is one branch in which we are the best judges, in which heresies may be taught, of so interesting a character to our own State and to the United States, as to make a duty in us to lay down the principles which shall be taught. It is that of government. Mr. Gilmer being withdrawn, we know not who his successor may be. He may be a Richmond lawyer, or one of that school of quondam federalism, now consolidation. It is our duty to guard against the dissemination of such principles among our youth, and the diffusion of that poison, by a previous prescription of the texts to be followed in their discourses.[16]

Even more important was the selection of the proper professor of law. Once again Jefferson was prepared to limit what we consider academic freedom in a cause so important and so precarious. Tolerant as he was,

Jefferson could not view with equanimity the possibility that some 'Richmond lawyer' might indoctrinate students with false political principles. To Madison he wrote, a few months before his death,

In the selection of our Law Professor we must be rigorously attentive to his political principles. You will recollect that before the Revolution, Coke Littleton was the universal elementary book of law students, and a sounder Whig never wrote, nor of profounder learning in the orthodox doctrines of the British constitution, or in what were called English liberties. You remember also that our lawyers were then all Whigs. But when his black-letter text, and uncouth but cunning learning got out of fashion, and the honeyed Mansfieldism of Blackstone became the students' hornbook, from that moment that profession (the nursery of our Congress) began to slide into toryism and nearly all the young brood of lawyers now are of that hue. They suppose themselves indeed to be Whigs, because they no longer know what Whigism or republicanism means. It is in our seminary that that vestal flame is to be kept alive; it is thence it is to spread anew over our sister States. If we are true and vigilant in our trust, within a dozen or twenty years a majority of our own legislature will be from one school, and many disciples will have carried its doctrines home with them to their several States, and will have leavened thus the whole mass.[17]

But Jefferson's arguments against judicial review were in vain, his plans for assuring doctrinal soundness in teaching were to be frustrated: Harvard and Justice Story [18] were to see to that.

The replies of the northern states to the Kentucky

and Virginia Resolutions were unmistakable indications of the hold that judicial review already had on the public mind. No need for state legislatures to trouble themselves—so said the legislators of Rhode Island, Vermont, New Hampshire, New York, and other northern states—the courts would take care of all constitutional questions.[19] It was an ominous prophecy—ominous not because faith in the courts was necessarily misplaced, but because it revealed already thus early that evasion of responsibility and that illogic which has characterized the public attitude towards this problem ever since that day.

With the passing years judicial review became ever more strongly entrenched. Not again, to be sure, was Marshall to invalidate a congressional act—not indeed for fifty-four years was there to be another such nullification. But in decision after decision the inferior and state courts as well as the Supreme Court did nullify acts of the states, and assert the authority of the judiciary to be the sole arbiter of the Constitution; the Commentaries of Kent [20] and Story [21] reaffirmed the dogma, and in time it became a part of our unwritten constitution.

Jefferson watched this process with malign dissatisfaction, and from Monticello went a steady stream of letters packed with exhaustive arguments, bitter diatribes, desperate appeals, against the encroachments of the judicial oligarchy. It was, he confessed, 'the great object of my fear . . . That body like gravity, ever acting, with noiseless foot, and unalarming advance, gaining ground step by step and holding what it gains, is ingulfing insidiously the special governments into the jaws of that which feeds them.' [22] It is 'the subtle corps of sappers and miners constantly working to undermine the foundations of our confederated fabric'; [23] it is 'an irresponsible body, working like gravity by night and by day . . . advancing its noiseless step like a thief.' [24] It was 'setting itself in opposition to the common sense of the nation,' [25] 'usurping legislation . . . practicing on the Constitution by inferences, analogies and sophisms,' [26] 'bidding defiance to the spirit of the whole nation,' [27] making the Constitution 'a mere thing of wax . . . which they may twist and shape into any form they please.' [28]

It was a losing fight, even when Taylor of Caroline [29] and Spencer Roane [30] joined in the fray. It has been, ever since, a losing fight. But it has been a useful one, for the axiom 'eternal vigilance is the price of liberty' applies not to the legislative and executive alone. We cannot overturn now the institution of judicial review, even if we would. Yet we may not lightly disregard the warnings and animadversions of the statesmen who contributed so largely both to constitutionalism and to democracy, where both are concerned. The theory and the history of judicial review are hackneyed subjects, yet some aspects of its application to majority rule and minority rights still bear re-examination.

For we have come to take this institution so completely for granted that we have lost sight of its real nature. Few of our political institutions have been more elaborately explained and documented; none, it is safe to say, is less understood.[31] Misunderstanding is no monopoly of conservatives who celebrate judicial review as a bulwark of republicanism; it distinguishes equally liberals who for the most part deprecate judicial intervention in the economic realm but rejoice exceedingly at judicial intervention on behalf of civil liberties. Neither group seems to appreciate the implications or the consequences of this unique institution. The dust of confusion hangs heavily over the discussions of the court reform and of the numerous Jehovah's Witnesses cases. In all the millions of words that have been poured over these issues, few touch reality. The court reform proposal of 1937 furnished the most promising opportunity offered our generation for an analysis of the relation of judicial review to democracy, but no such analysis was vouchsafed us: the gallant throng of experts who trooped down to Washington to testify to the merits and demerits of S. 1392 managed to talk about almost everything but that.[32] The clash between majority and minority of the Supreme Court in the flag salute and other Jehovah's Witnesses cases revealed clearly enough the issue of the reconciliation of 'the conflicting claims of liberty and authority,' but a hundred commentators succeeded with wonderful agility in ignoring the issue. Indeed so general has been the failure to confront realistically the problem of judicial review that we are forced to the conclusion that it is rooted in ignorance or confusion rather than in timidity or circumspection.

How can it be said that the problem of judicial review is the problem of democracy? A moment's reflection on the institution will clarify the statement. The function —and effect—of judicial review is to give or deny judicial sanction to an act passed by a majority of a legislative body and approved by an executive. Every act adjudicated by the court has not only been ratified by a majority, but it has—in theory and we must suppose in fact—been subject to scrutiny in regard to its conformity with the Constitution. In support of every act, therefore, is not only a majority vote for its wisdom but a majority vote for its constitutionality.

Where the question of constitutionality is raised the judiciary subjects the act anew to scrutiny—theoretically on constitutional grounds alone, never on expediency. Where it concludes that the act involved is contrary to the Constitution, it so holds. In doing this it, of course, opposes its own opinion on constitutionality to that of the other two branches of the government. We can put the situation even more sharply: the one non-elective and non-removable element in the government rejects the conclusions on constitutionality arrived at by the two elective and removable branches.

A further observation is pertinent. Obviously the political majorities are never aware—and would never admit—that they are violating the Constitution. There are rarely, if ever, clear-cut instances where wilful majorities deliberately ride down constitutional barriers. There are rarely, if ever, real instances analogous to the hypothetical instances that Marshall conjured up in Marbury *v.* Madison—and which have been exploited by champions of judicial review ever since. Popular notions to the contrary notwithstanding—and I shall have something to say of this later—our legislative bodies, both state and national, have been throughout our history profoundly conservative and constitution-minded. In every instance of challenged legislation we may assume that the majority responsible for the law believed that it was legislating in harmony with the Constitution. If this should seem odd, to the lay mind, we may add that in most instances some judges have been found to agree with them! This is true of the majorities that enacted the Alien and Sedition laws, that passed Reconstruction legislation, that fabricated the New Deal; it is true equally of the majorities in state legislatures that passed workmen's compensation laws, maximum-hour and minimum-wage laws, even anti-evolution laws.

The real question, of course, is not that of blind or malicious majorities riding down constitutional guarantees, but of differing interpretations of the meaning of the Constitution. The crucial question is not so much whether an act does or does not conform to the Constitution, but who shall judge regarding its conformity? For it is still true, as Bishop Hoadly said over two centuries ago: 'Whoever hath an *absolute authority* to interpret any written or spoken laws, it is *He* who is truly the *Law-Giver* to all intents and purposes, and not the person who first wrote or spoke them.' [33]

What is the argument for judicial rather than legislative or executive interpretations of the Constitution and laws? The orthodox answer is familiar enough. In the words of Marshall, 'it is emphatically the province and duty of the judicial department to say what the law is.' [34] That is the essence of judicial business—to know the law and to know the Constitution, and in this the other departments cannot hope to compete. But not only are the courts peculiarly fitted to interpret the law but—and here we come to a most persuasive argument—they alone are independent and unbiased, their judgment alone is to be trusted.

These are large claims—confidently made and boldly maintained but scarcely susceptible of proof. It is possible, however, to challenge both of them; it is possible, too, to enter a demurrer—to plead that even if the claims are sound, the wisdom of judicial review in a democratic system is by no means established.

That judges—especially judges of our highest courts—are more learned in the law than legislators or executives will not be gainsaid. Is the observation relevant? Does the issue of constitutionality customarily involve legal erudition? Have acts of Congress—or of state legislatures—frequently been challenged on the basis of provisions of our constitutions so intricate that great learning is required for their comprehension? There have been examples of this, to be sure. But for the most part judicial rejection of legislative acts has not been an exercise of learning but of discretion. As Justice Holmes said back in 1896, 'the true grounds of decision are considerations of policy and of social advantage, and it is vain to suppose that solutions can be attained merely by logic and the general propositions of law which nobody disputes.' [35]

Indeed if we turn for simplicity to the federal scene, we shall find that acts which have encountered judicial invalidation have in every instance required the interpretation of vague and ambiguous clauses of the Constitution—clauses whose meaning is not to be determined by legal research but by 'considerations of policy.' Thus when the Supreme Court asserts that the Congress has not authority to regulate slavery in the Territories, to authorize legal tender, to impose a tax upon incomes, to prohibit yellow-dog contracts, to deny the channels of interstate commerce to the products of child labor, to fix minimum wages for women in the District of Columbia, to lay taxes for the purpose of regulating agricultural production—when it does all these things it is not applying clear-cut provisions of the Constitution but interpreting vague phrases like 'regulation of commerce,' 'general welfare,' 'due process of law,' and so forth. And when the court interprets these and similar phrases it does not so much exploit legal learning as exercise discretion.

I do not suggest that learning is not an essential quality in a judge—though our admiration, it may be noted, lingers with Marshall rather than with Story—but I do submit that questions that have evoked judicial nullification of majority will have turned on considerations of policy rather than of law, and that on these questions the legal learning of the legislative and executive departments has been entirely adequate.

What of the other assumption—that judges, alone, can be trusted to act independently, objectively, and dispassionately on questions of constitutionality? The assumption that legislators ever consciously permit passion or prejudice to influence their judgment where the Constitution is involved is, of course, intolerable, so what we are concerned with is unconscious bias, and the argument is that judges have less of this than legislators. The contemporary school of legal realists has dealt very harshly with the whole notion of judicial objectivity—has, perhaps, gone too far in support of the thesis that judicial opinions are largely the product of personal and environmental imponderables.[36] But if it is an exaggeration to say that judicial opinion depends on judicial digestion, it will not be denied that the 'mechanical' or 'phonographic' theory of jurisprudence has been completely discredited.

It may not be without interest to recall that Jefferson —who was himself a lawyer and a very successful one— did not subscribe to the theory of judicial objectivity. He had seen judges, at the time of the Alien and Sedition hysteria, use the bench as a political hustings; he had suffered from the 'court-packing' episode of 1800; he had protested, with others, the 'political statesmanship' of Marshall and his brother Story, and he was thoroughly disillusioned. 'The federalists,' he wrote indignantly, shortly after his accession to the presidency, 'have retired into the judiciary as a stronghold. There the remains of federalism are to be preserved and fed from the treasury and from that battery all the works of republicanism are to be beaten down and erased.' [37] Our judges, he explained to William Jarvis,

> are as honest as other men—and not more so. They have, with others, the same passion for party, for power, and the privileges of their corps. Their maxim is 'boni judicia est ampliare jurisdictionem,' and their power more dangerous as they are in office for life, and not responsible, as other functionaries are, to the elective control.[38]

Marshall was 'a crafty chief judge who sophisticates the law to his mind, by the turn of his own reasoning.' [39] And, in his Autobiography, he concluded,

> It is not enough that honest men are appointed Judges. All know the influence of interest on the mind of man, and how unconsciously his judgment is warped by that influence. To this bias add that of the esprit de corps, of their peculiar maxim and creed, that 'it is the office of a good judge to enlarge his jurisdiction,' and the absence of responsibility; and how can we expect impartial decision . . .[40]

All this is historically interesting rather than conclusive, but it is interesting, too, to note that these charges have been echoed, in one form or another, by

Jackson, Lincoln, Bryan, and both Roosevelts, and that from dissenting members of the court have come similar criticisms, less acrimonious but not less emphatic. It is judges who have charged that the court indulges in 'judicial legislation,' warned that 'fear of socialism' unduly influences decisions, protested against 'a tortured construction of the Constitution.'[41] And it is difficult to read such opinions as those of Story in the Charles River Bridge Company case, Taney in the Dred Scott case, Field in the Income Tax case, Peckham in the Lochner case, McReynolds in the Gold Clause cases—to name only a few of the more notorious—and avoid the conclusion that judges are sometimes swayed by considerations other than those of constitutional logic.

But if it cannot be shown that superior learning is an essential ingredient of judicial review or objectivity a peculiar possession of judges, what shall we say of the arguments supporting that institution? Is it possible that Jefferson's strictures—looked upon by many as an amiable, or merely tolerable, aberration—were valid? Is it possible to challenge judicial review (always as a restriction on majority will rather than as a harmonizer of the federal system) on the basic ground that it has not, in fact, justified itself?

For the most part consideration of this institution has gone on in the rarified atmosphere of theory and hypothesis, but our question is one not of theory but of fact. It is commonly taken for granted that courts decide rightly all questions of constitutional law, that they curb majority will only to protect minority rights, that their intervention has saved the Constitution from impairment or destruction. A realistic examination of the operation of judicial review in the federal field will not sustain these assumptions. It is safe to say that had there never been an instance of judicial nullification of a congressional act, our constitutional system would be essentially the same as it is today. For most of the judicial nullifications of federal legislation have been cancelled out by amendment, by new—and more acceptable—legislation, or, more frequently, by judicial reversal. It is safe to say, further, that the judicial record in the important—and controversial—field of personal liberties is practically barren—again, as far as federal legislation is concerned. In short, if we had to depend upon the courts rather than upon Congress and the President for maintaining our constitutional system and protecting personal liberties, we would be in an awkward position. The fact is, of course, that there are very few instances where the Congress has threatened the integrity of the constitutional system or the guarantee of the Bill of Rights.

A simple analysis of the actual incidence of judicial review in the field of congressional legislation is perhaps the most effective support to these generalizations.[42] There have been, altogether, some seventy-five instances of such judicial nullification.[43] About half of these have been of a technical—we may say, of a highly technical—nature. The number of consequential cases has been comparatively small—though important quite out of proportion to their number. It will not do too much injustice to the history or significance of judicial review to characterize these cases briefly:

Marbury *v.* Madison [44]—really one of the most technical cases but significant because it was the first instance of judicial nullification of congressional legislation—rejected a congressional authorization to the Supreme Court to issue a writ of mandamus. The only practical effect of the decision was to deny Marbury the job to which the court held he was morally entitled. The implications of the decision both with respect to the presidential power of removal and with respect to the jurisdiction of the court were subsequently seriously modified by the court itself. The provision nullified—section 13 of the Judiciary Act of 1789—threatened neither the integrity of the Constitution nor the rights of persons.

Dred Scott *v.* Sanford [45] nullified a provision of the Missouri Compromise already repealed, and announced that the Congress had no authority to prohibit slavery in the Territories—a decision indubitably erroneous and shortly reversed by congressional action.[46] The enduring importance of the decision is to be found, rather, in the announcement that the due-process clause of the fifth and by implication the fourteenth amendment had a substantive as well as a procedural significance.[47]

Hepburn *v.* Griswold [48] denied to the Congress the right to make paper money legal tender for the payment of debts contracted prior to the enactment of the law. The decision—palpably erroneous—was reversed the following year.

Ex parte Garland [49] held that an act forbidding a person who had participated in the rebellion from practicing before the Supreme Court was 'ex post facto,' partook of attainder, and qualified the presidential pardon, and was therefore void. Dubious as was this construction (four judges held that the requirement of loyalty was not a punishment but merely a proper qualification) it constitutes perhaps the best example of judicial protection of personal rights from congressional impairment in the whole of our history.

United States *v.* Klein [50] nullified an act of Congress that denied to persons who had participated in the rebellion, the right to sue for the recovery of confiscated property, even though they had subsequently been pardoned. The decision may have broadened the scope of the pardoning power, mitigated the consequences of technical treason, and benefited a few well-to-do Southerners.

Collector *v.* Day [51]—as well as the later Evans *v.* Gore [52] and Miles *v.* Graham [53]—exempted state and federal judges from payment of income taxes. The effect was, in the words of Justice Holmes, to make judges 'a privileged class free from bearing their share of the cost of the institutions upon which their well-being if not their life depends.' Both the later decisions have since been reversed.

A long series of cases having to do with the interpretation of laws designed to effectuate the provisions of the Thirteenth, Fourteenth, and Fifteenth Amendments may be considered together. United States *v.* Reese,[54] United States *v.* Harris,[55] Civil Rights Cases,[56] Baldwin *v.* Franks,[57] James *v.* Bowman,[58] Hodges *v.* United States,[59] and Butts *v.* Merchants Transportation Co.[60] all in effect nullified the efforts of Congress to put teeth into these Amendments by ruling that Congress may prohibit only such discrimination against Negroes as flows from state—not private—action, and that the rights of Negroes which are protected are those rights only which derive from citizenship in the United States as distinct from state citizenship—a vague and limited category.

Monongahela Navigation Co. *v.* United States [61] held that the determination of the measure of compensation in the purchase of a public utility franchise was a judicial, not a legislative, function. It was one of the earliest of that long series of opinions—most of them relating to state laws—which transferred rate making from the legislatures to the courts—a responsibility the courts are now as eager to evade as they were once to embrace.

Pollock *v.* Farmers' Loan and Trust Co.[62] invalidated the income-tax law of 1894. It remains, with Dred Scott, the most unfortunate of all exhibitions of judicial review. The opinion reversed earlier decisions and was, in turn, reversed by the Sixteenth Amendment. Its practical effect was merely to delay for almost twenty years the application of a system of taxation universally recognized as sound.

Wong Wing *v.* United States [63] held invalid a statute granting authority to a United States Commissioner rather than to a jury to try Chinese alleged to be unlawfully in the country. That the Chinese aliens would receive a fairer trial from a jury than from a Commissioner is not clear; but in any event the decision is memorable because it is one of the two (*ex parte* Garland is the other) in which the court may be said to have protected the rights of persons against congressional assault.

Adair *v.* United States [64] voided that part of the Erdman Act which was designed to outlaw yellow-dog contracts in interstate commerce. It represented a retreat from the long-established Marshall tradition of the interpretation of the commerce clause as well as a stunning setback to reform in the field of labor legislation. It furnished the inspiration and justification for outlawing similar state laws and thus, in effect, sustained the yellow-dog contract for a quarter-century. It has recently been overruled.

So, too, the Employers' Liability Cases [65] rejected reliance upon the commerce clause as authority for establishing employers' liability for interstate carriers where the liability was not clearly confined to the interstate activities of those carriers. A second act, which attempted to conform to this limitation by limiting benefits to employees suffering injury while actually engaged in interstate commerce, has required the court to devote some fifty opinions to the vain attempt to distinguish clearly between railroad employment which is interstate and that which is intrastate in character.

Keller *v.* United States [66] held that congressional control over immigration does not extend to the punishment of those who exploit immigrant girls for purposes of prostitution. And, in a comparable field, Matter of Heff [67] decided that the Congress could not punish the illegal sale of liquor to Indians if the Indians were at the same time citizens. Eleven years later the court, affirming that 'citizenship is not incompatible with tribal existence or continued guardianship,' reversed this decision.

Newberry *v.* United States [68] decided that party primaries are not part of elections and that the Congress therefore does not have authority to prohibit corrupt practices in primaries. The opinion has recently been seriously modified—perhaps reversed—by United States *v.* Classic.[69]

Hammer *v.* Dagenhart [70] overturned a child-labor law on the ground that regulation of commerce does not extend to the prohibition of the products of child labor in interstate commerce. The decision has recently been reversed. Bailey *v.* Drexel Furniture Company [71] nullified the attempt of Congress to tax the products of child labor out of existence as an improper exercise of the taxing power.

Eisner *v.* Macomber [72] partly defeated the purpose

of the income tax amendment by deciding that a stock dividend was not income within the meaning of that amendment.

Adkins *v.* Children's Hospital [73] invoked the esoteric due-process clause of the Fifth Amendment to nullify a congressional effort to fix minimum wages for women in the District of Columbia. Such legislation was, the court asserted, an improper interference with liberty of contract. The decision has since been reversed.

United States *v.* Cohen Grocery Co.[74] held that part of the Lever war-time agricultural act which prohibited 'unfair or unreasonable' rates or charges void because too vague. The rebuke was pertinent, but it is equally pertinent to remark that legislative recourse to vague phrases of this nature has been encouraged by reliance upon judicial legislation in the premises. If the courts are prepared to decide the meaning of such terms as 'just,' 'reasonable,' 'fair,' and so forth, why should the legislature bother? [75]

Hill *v.* Wallace [76] announced that the penalty tax on trading in grain futures was not authorized by the commerce clause of the Constitution.

Myers *v.* United States [77] invalidated—sixty years later—a reconstruction law designed to limit the President's power of removal. If the decision was correct, the implications of Marbury *v.* Madison were not, but the more recent Humphrey's Executor [78] opinion suggests some reservations regarding the finality of the Myers decision.

United States *v.* Constantine [79] invalidated a heavy

penalty tax imposed upon liquor dealers carrying on their traffic in violation of state or local laws, on the ground that the repeal of the Eighteenth Amendment had removed the subject from federal jurisdiction. The only interests served were those of states' rights and bootleggers.

The New Deal cases are almost too recent and too familiar to justify rehearsal. United States *v.* Butler [80] voided the AAA on the somewhat confused grounds of an improper interpretation of the general welfare and of the tax clauses of the Constitution; Perry *v.* United States [81] held the repudiation of the gold obligation in government bonds was both illegal and immoral, but that as no one was hurt, no one could collect damages. Schechter *v.* United States [82] struck down the NRA both because it was not a proper exercise of the commerce power and because it was an improper delegation of power by Congress to the Executive. This latter argument was the basis, too, of the invalidation of an act authorizing the President to regulate the transportation of 'hot oil.' [83] Railroad Retirement Board *v.* Alton Railroad,[84] outlawing a system of railway retirement pensions, was a further limitation upon the commerce power; Louisville *v.* Radford [85] and Ashton *v.* Cameron County [86] restrained the authority of Congress over bankruptcies and over the readjustment of municipal indebtedness. Carter *v.* Carter Coal Co.[87] sought to remove the regulation of the coal industry from the domain of congressional control.

This is the record. It is familiar enough to students of our constitutional law; less familiar, perhaps, to the layman who, not unnaturally, supposes the court continuously intervening to protect fundamental rights of life, liberty, and property from congressional assault. It discloses not a single case, in a century and a half, where the Supreme Court has protected freedom of speech, press, assembly, or petition against congressional attack. It reveals no instance (with the possible exception of the dubious Wong Wing case) where the court has intervened on behalf of the underprivileged—the Negro, the alien, women, children, workers, tenant-farmers. It reveals, on the contrary, that the court has effectively intervened again and again to defeat congressional efforts to free slaves, guarantee civil rights to Negroes, to protect workingmen, outlaw child labor, assist hard-pressed farmers, and to democratize the tax system. From this analysis the Congress, and not the courts, emerges as the instrument for the realization of the guarantees of the bill of rights.

Our examination, then, of the theory and practice of judicial review, of congressional legislation, affords some basis for accepting the Jeffersonian rather than the Hamiltonian view of this institution. Whatever the logical support for the theory, it cannot be found in the philosophy of democracy if by democracy we mean majority rule; whatever the practical justification, it cannot be found in the defense of fundamental rights against the assaults of misguided or desperate majorities.

Almost every instance of judicial nullification of congressional acts appears, now, to have been a mistaken one. In many—perhaps in most—instances the mistake has been (after a decent interval) conceded and corrected by the court itself. In other instances it has been rectified by the operation of public opinion. The conclusion is almost inevitable that judicial review in this realm has been a drag upon administrative efficiency and upon democracy.

Yet the fundamental problem remains. If we are to give free reign to majority rule, where shall we turn for protection of minority rights? Is there any lasting assurance that the majority, unawed by judicial restraints, will respect those rights? It is to what we may call the Jeffersonian answer to this question that we will direct our attention.

III

The Jeffersonian Solution

'The people,' a distinguished contemporary statesman has said in a phrase already classic, 'have no right to do wrong.'[1] It is at least suggestive that Eamon de Valera, who has fought pretty consistently for his people and who regards himself as a democrat, should have found it necessary to invoke the techniques of totalitarianism to prevent the people from 'doing wrong.' And it is a characteristic of almost every anti-democratic philosophy that it purports to serve the welfare of the people but refuses to trust the judgment of the people on questions affecting their welfare.

We concluded our consideration of the incidence of judicial review of federal laws with the query, What assurance do we have, if we remove the judicial restraints, that majorities will not disregard the 'laws of Nature and Nature's God,' destroy minority rights, and bring down upon themselves the whole fine structure of constitutionalism? What guarantee is there, in short, that the people, if conceded the right, will not do wrong?

Those familiar with British history might make a very interesting answer to this question, for in Britain the people have had the right to do wrong for some time, now, and have not exercised it in any notorious fashion. But we may profitably confine ourselves to American history, which is sufficiently illuminating. And we must observe first that, as regards the American constitutional system, the question is a leading and a misleading one. The judiciary is not the only check upon majority will. The supposition that the removal of the judicial check would leave our government an unlimited one is entirely erroneous, and the confusion of majority rule with despotism or even anarchy almost deliberately malicious.

Our constitutional system, as has already been observed, is one of checks and balances: these have already been noted. It is sometimes forgotten that our political system is one of checks and balances too. Anyone who has followed the slow and tortuous course of a major public issue—the poll tax, for example, or neutrality, through the arena of public opinion, into the party conventions and caucuses, into the halls of Congress and the rooms of appropriate committees, knows how much of delay, of balance, of compromise, is implicit in our political machinery. A good part of our politics, indeed, seems to be concerned with reconciling majority and minority will, class hostilities, sectional differences, the divergent interests of producer and consumer, of agriculture and labor, of creditor and debtor, of city and country, of tax-payer and tax-beneficiary, of the military and the civilian. In small issues as in great, the result is generally a compromise. Democracy, in short, whether from instinct or from necessity, furnishes its own checks and balances—quite aside from such as may be provided in written constitutions.

Indeed it might plausibly be argued that it is one of the major advantages of democracy over other forms of government that it alone can indulge in the luxury of tolerating minority and dissenting groups because it alone has developed the technique for dealing with them.[2] It is sometimes charged as a criticism of democracy that it cannot act speedily and effectively in an emergency—as can totalitarian or despotic governments. The charge is not sound—as witness the efficiency of our own democracy in the spring of 1933 or the winter of 1941-2—but it is true that in a democracy it requires a real emergency to produce prompt and effective action.

But there is this to be said of the checks and balances of democratic politics—that they are natural, not artificial; that they are flexible rather than rigid; that they can yield to public opinion and to necessity. They do, sometimes, enable the majority to ride down the minority; they do, far more frequently, enable the minority to delay and defeat the majority. But the responsibility in all this is with the people themselves—where it belongs. Where they indulge their apathy, their carelessness, their blindness, they pay the price, and it is right that they should pay the price. As the fault is theirs, so, too, the remedy. Where issues appear sufficiently important the majority can have its way even against the recalcitrance of minorities who take refuge in the labyrinths of our party and our legislative systems. But against minorities entrenched in the judiciary there is no effective appeal except through the complicated and slow process of constitutional amendment. Here it is true today as it was in 1801 that the minority can 'retire into the judiciary as a stronghold,' and 'from that battery' beat down the works of republicanism.

A majority rule system, then, such as ours, is not a system of unlimited government either in theory, in law, or in practice. To the formal limits of the Constitution are added the informal limits of politics. With this in mind we can return to our original question: Is there any reason to suppose that majorities so limited would invade minority rights if it were not for the obstacles interposed by the courts? Or may we advance with equal plausibility the assertion that majorities can be trusted, without judicial assistance, to govern in accordance with the law and to respect minority rights, and that—with full realization of all the risks involved—training in such governance is essential to the maturing of democracy?

Scores of philosophers and historians have attempted to answer these questions, but almost always they have addressed themselves to theory rather than to fact. But answers—I will not say conclusive answers—are to be found in the realm of fact. We are fortunate in having here, in the United States, the most elaborate political laboratory in all history and one whose findings have been pretty fully recorded. Popular government has been a going concern here, in one form or another, for about three hundred years. We have, for our edification, the history of the experience of the thirteen colonies, of the national government, and of thirteen to forty-eight states, for varying periods of time. What does this record reveal?

It reveals a stability, a respect for law, a zeal for individual and minority rights that cannot be equalled, it is safe to say, by any other type of government in the history of western civilization. In all this period—and in all these governments—there has not been a single example of lawless revolution.[3] In all this period, and for all these governments, there has been but one example of a deliberate and sustained effort by a majority to subvert constitutional rights or oppress a minority,[4] the determination of Southern whites to frustrate the Fourteenth and Fifteenth Amendments, in so far as these attempted to assure political and social rights to Negroes. In all this period and for all these governments there have been comparatively few instances of even temporary aberration.

These are very sweeping generalizations and I do not pretend that I should be able to substantiate them, state by state, year by year, law by law. But our national history has been fully recorded and many earnest students have painstakingly compiled the histories of their states, and it is a reasonable assumption that revolutionary violence, attempts to subvert the Constitution, suppression of individual liberties, would appear in the record. And I submit that anyone who combs our national and state histories to find instances of legislative or executive lawlessness will find but meagre results.

To Jefferson in Paris, in 1786 and 1787, came—in somewhat garbled form—the story of the Shays' uprising. The conclusion of most scholars, now, is that this uprising was amply justified and was by no means directed to the overthrow of government.[5] Jefferson could not know this; he assumed that the outbreak was, actually, a lawless one; yet he was puzzled at the frenzy that seemed to possess the conservatives. What, after all, was such an uprising but 'proof that the people have liberty enough, and I could not wish them less than they have. If the happiness of the mass of the people can be secured at the expense of a little tempest now and then, or even of a little blood, it will be a precious purchase.' [6]

God forbid we should ever be twenty years without such a rebellion. The people cannot be all, and always, well informed. The part which is wrong, will be discontented, in proportion to the importance of the facts they misconceive. If they remain quiet under such misconceptions, it is a lethargy, the forerunner of death to the public liberty . . .

What signify a few lives lost in a century or two? The tree of liberty must be refreshed from time to time with the blood of patriots and tyrants. It is its natural manure.[7]

This would do as a starter, but it did not cover the whole ground. Jefferson hastened to console himself—and comfort his friends—with reassuring mathematical formulae. Thirteen states independent for eleven years; that comes to one rebellion in every century and a half. What other nation has so good a record? [8] Years later, in his prolonged and amiable disputation with John Adams, he returned to this plausible formula: 'From fifteen to twenty legislatures of our own' he wrote, in 1813, 'in action for thirty years past, have proved that no fears of an equalization of property are to be apprehended from them.' [9] What fun he would have had, now, with forty-eight states of various ages to conjure with!

This approach to the problem has a romantic simplicity about it, yet it is fundamentally sound. For the history of the American nation is after all the most effective answer that can be made to the charge that democracies are unstable and subversive, that they oppress minorities, yield their liberties to dictators, use government as an instrument for levelling society and economy, crush individualism, require conformity, elevate mediocrity, and lead to all the other evils that critics from Adams to Spengler have prophesied.

I am not unaware of certain chapters in our history that would appear to support the theories of the critics.

The maintenance and defense of the institutions of slavery is not one which we can now regard with satisfaction—but it may be suggested that the institution rooted itself in the least democratic section of the country, that the most profound of Southern political thinkers recognized that majority rule was incompatible with its perpetuation and formulated a philosophy designed to circumvent the inconvenience of majority rule. The determination of the white majority of the South, since the Civil War, to 'keep the Negro in his place' is again one difficult to reconcile with my theory that democracies are not inimical to freedom. Perhaps the only relevant observations on a subject so large, so complex, and so delicate, are that the processes of education upon which Jefferson so largely relied have not gone far enough; that the local majorities do not represent national majorities; that social and economic security for the whites—surely part of the Jeffersonian program—might be expected to encourage a different attitude; and that judicial intervention has, in any event, been unavailing or ineffective.

Nor am I forgetting political episodes that might lend support to the notion that democracies run to dictatorships or that they are inimical to liberty: the episodes of the Tweed Ring in New York, of the Cameron and the Quay machines in Pennsylvania, of the triumph of the Fergusons in Texas, of Huey Long in Louisiana, of Talmadge in Georgia. I shall not maneuver myself into the awkward position of defending or even extenuating these displays of machine or boss rule. But of them all we can, I think, say that their threat to real democracy and even to liberty arose from ignorance and confusion rather than from any philosophical antipathy,[10] that they did not succeed in destroying either democracy or liberty, and that they were temporary—and exceptional.

More serious, in the indictment of majority rule, is the long list of laws materially impairing civil liberties that have come from all of our state legislatures, especially in the last quarter of a century. A cumulative list of these might well dishearten even the most optimistic Jeffersonian. Censorship laws, anti-evolution laws, teachers' oath laws, flag-salute laws, red-flag laws, anti-syndicalist, anti-socialist, anti-communist laws, sedition and criminal-anarchy laws, anti-contraceptive information laws—these and others come all too readily to mind. The New York legislature purged itself of socialists; the Massachusetts legislature imposed loyalty oaths on teachers; the Oregon legislature outlawed private schools; the Nebraska legislature forbade the teaching of German in public schools; the Tennessee legislature prohibited the teaching of evolution; the Pennsylvania legislature authorized the requirement of a flag-salute from school children; the Louisiana legislature imposed a discriminatory tax upon newspapers; the West Virginia legislature protected future generations by making unlawful any teachings 'of ideals to those now or henceforth existing under the constitution and laws of this State.' The list could be extended indefinitely.[11]

It is here, if anywhere, that judicial review has justified itself. In a long and distinguished series of decisions the courts have cushioned the shock of these acts upon the state and federal bills of rights. Some they have, perforce, accepted; some they have interpreted so as to ameliorate their incidence; a great many they have nullified. The record of these nullifications is gratifying to every one who cherishes the great Anglo-American tradition of personal liberties: De Jonge *v.* Oregon, Pierce *v.* Society of Sisters, Nixon *v.* Herndon, Fiske *v.* Kansas, Stromberg *v.* California, Thornhill *v.* Alabama, Herndon *v.* Lowry, Chambers *v.* Florida, Powell *v.* Alabama, Near *v.* Minnesota, Hague *v.* C.I.O., Lovell *v.* Griffen—to name only the most familiar.[12]

And what shall the Jeffersonian say of judicial review when confronted by this record of judicial intervention on behalf of those very liberties which Jefferson regarded as the end of government? (To secure these rights, governments are instituted among men.) Is it possible to make a distinction between judicial review of legislative acts having to do with ordinary administrative or economic matters and those having to do with what we call 'civil liberties'? There is strong—and growing—support for such a contention.[13] The presumption of constitutionality, it is argued, should hold for all ordinary laws, and the courts should refrain from interfering in mere economic experiments, however unwise. But with laws that might limit, in any way—numerically, socially, intellectually—the power of the electorate to reconsider, that presumption no longer holds. Thus Justice Stone in U.S. *v.* Carolene Products Co.[14] listed several types of laws that 'restrict those political processes which can ordinarily be expected to bring about repeal of undesirable legislation' as worthy of 'more exacting judicial scrutiny'—restrictions on the right to vote, on the dissemination of information, on interference with political organizations, on prohibition of peaceable assembly, on particular religious practices, on racial minorities.

The logic behind such a distinction is obvious enough. A legislative mistake in fixing rates, in taxation, in organizing administrative bureaus, in limiting hours or conditions of labor—can be corrected by a subsequent legislature representing the electorate that first authorized the law. But a law that changes the electorate or that denies it access to proper information cannot be reviewed by the same electorate. Legislation therefore that in any way affects the quantity or the quality of the body politic is in a peculiar position and must be subject to peculiar scrutiny.

Certainly there would seem to be a persuasive argument here for judicial review. But grant the desirability or the necessity of calling in the judiciary to protect civil liberties, and we concede that the majority is not to be trusted in what is perhaps the most important field of its legislative activity. If we are compelled to make that concession here, in a matter so vitally affecting the liberty and happiness of every member of society, then we might indeed despair of democracy.

But before we embrace a conclusion which, Jefferson wrote, would force him to believe 'either that there is no God, or that he is a malevolent being,' [15] there are several considerations that command our attention. And first it may be suggested that few of these laws apparently striking at freedom of speech or the press or at minority rights are clear violations of specific constitutional provisions. Most of them are border-line cases. They involve—like the recent flag-salute ordinances—a nice adjustment of powers granted and powers prohibited. They involve interpretation of clauses of the Constitution inevitably ambiguous—clauses like 'due process of law' or 'deprivation of liberty' or even 'abridging' freedom of speech or of the press. It is instructive to note that the court more often finds it necessary to sustain these laws than possible to nullify them.

And this brings us to a second consideration—namely, that the distinction between so-called civil-liberties laws and other laws is by no means clear-cut, that it may even be artificial and misleading. We incline, of course, to a delusive simplification of these matters. Was the Louisiana law imposing a heavy tax upon newspapers with large circulations an exercise of the taxing powers, or was it a badly concealed attempt to penalize opposition papers and thus an interference with freedom of the press? [16] Was the ordinance requiring special permits for the distribution of handbills a proper exercise of the right to prevent littering the streets—or was it an attack upon the rights of a religious minority? [17] Is the law forbidding doctors to give out contraceptive information a proper exercise of the police power—or an illegal interference with the rights of the medical profession? [18] Is the ordinance requiring a flag-salute from school children a proper exercise of control over education—or is it an assault upon the guarantees of the First Amendment? [19]

In these, and in similar cases, the legislatures may have been animated by an entirely genuine desire to cope with financial or with police problems properly under their control. Legislatures do, after all, control taxation; they do, after all, possess that vague but convenient body of authority known as the police power: Who is to judge the propriety of the exercise of these powers? Who can be sure that when New York outlaws the manufacture of tobacco in tenement houses it is not actually and honestly attempting to regulate the public health and not attempting to harass business? [20] Who can be sure that when Illinois attempts to prohibit the night-work of women in industrial plants it is not honestly attempting to protect the health and morals of women and not gratuitously interfering with the liberty of contract? [21] Are we prepared to deny the sincerity of our legislative and executive bodies, or must we not, in a democracy, give them the benefit of that doubt—what lawyers call the presumption of constitutionality?

Or, conversely, it may be asked, is legislation regulating the hours and wages of workers, the practices or malpractices of trade unions, the relations between farm-owner and tenant, between creditor and debtor, legislation in the broad field of education—is all this less relevant, in actuality, to personal liberties than so-called personal liberty legislation? I should suggest that the distinction which is so glibly made is actually an unreal one and that a rejection of judicial review in one field and an acquiescence in it in another is not wholly logical.

There is a third consideration which we cannot ignore because it closely affects the nature of majority will. That is that legislation apparently violating personal liberties is inspired not by hostility to those rights but —generally—by a sincere but misguided desire to preserve them.

What we have here is not malice but confusion—the kind of confusion displayed by the Dies and the Kerr committees today. Members of these committees doubtless believe that Mr. William E. Dodd Jr., or Mr. Robert Morss Lovett entertains ideas inimical to our system of government—just as Mr. William E. Dodd Jr. and Mr. Robert Morss Lovett doubtless believe that Mr. Dies and Mr. Kerr entertain ideas inimical to our government. The whole discussion, which can be followed in the pages of the Congressional Record, is wonderfully illuminating. The point is that in almost every instance that legislators have infringed upon personal rights they have been animated by zeal for democracy and for liberty as they understood these things. Follow the legislative history of almost any of these acts—of the teachers' oath bills or the anti-syndicalism bills or the flag-salute bills and you will find that they have been supported by patriotic organizations like the American Legion or the Daughters of the American Revolution and that the arguments advanced have stressed the necessity of preserving inviolable the principles of the Declaration of Independence and of the Constitution. The explanation, as sage old Benjamin Franklin said about an analogous situation, is in 'distracted noddles.' And the way to deal with these is through discussion and education, not coercion.

A fourth observation which must be made in connection with judicial review of civil-liberties legislation—and it applies with some force to judicial review in general—is that it tends to substitute legal for political considerations, tends to confuse the technical question of constitutionality with the general political question of wisdom. As Mr. Justice Frankfurter warned us almost two decades ago:

> The tendency of focusing attention on constitutionality is to make constitutionality synonymous with propriety; to regard a law as all right so long as it is 'constitutional.' Such an attitude is a great enemy of liberalism. Particularly in legislation affecting freedom of thought and freedom of speech, much that is highly illiberal would be clearly constitutional . . . Here is ample warning to the liberal forces that the real battles of liberalism are not won in the Supreme Court.[22]

The real battles of liberalism are not to be won in any court. If we make constitutionality the test of civil-rights legislation we are pretty sure to lose our case, for it will not be difficult for the ingenuity of legislators—if they are so inclined—so to draft their laws as to surmount mere judicial barriers. Furthermore, we must remember that there is no automatic judicial review in our system. The constitutionality of many—probably of most—laws is not subjected to judicial scrutiny; even in laws of a highly dubious character it may take a decade or more before a judicial test can be arranged. The criterion, in any event, is an artificial one. It tends to distract attention from the real issues, places an improper responsibility upon the courts, and encourages government by litigation instead of government by political machinery. No, the place to meet, and to defeat, unwise or unconstitutional legislation is in the legislature or in the arena of public opinion.

And this brings us to the final and, I think, the most important consideration. That has to do with the long-range effect of the appeal to the judiciary instead of to the good sense of the people. Granted that majorities—like courts—are liable to error, how is that error to be cured and how is the repetition of that error best to be avoided? Is it not reasonable to suppose that majorities, like individuals, learn by their mistakes, and that only the lessons learned by experience make a lasting impression.

The impatient liberal, confronted with some example

of legislative stupidity or of injustice, is eager for immediate action. This 'quick surge of angry sympathy for men and women believed to have been wrongly hurt is,' as one student has written [23] 'our noblest badge of civilization.' But, he adds, the 'tendency to think in terms of the particular case' is 'one of the great obstacles to clear thinking.' For the remedy for the particular case is an appeal to the courts. The court may nullify the offensive legislation, but would not more be gained if the question were raised and agitated in the political instead of the judicial arena? The tendency to decide issues of personal liberty in the judicial arena alone has the effect of lulling the people into apathy towards issues that are fundamentally their concern, with the comforting notion that the courts will take care of personal and minority rights. It effectively removes these issues from the arena of public discussion and thus deprives democracy of the inestimable benefit of experimentation. As James Bradley Thayer pointed out over a generation ago:

> Great and, indeed, inestimable as are the advantages in a popular government of this conservative influence—the power of the judiciary to disregard unconstitutional legislation,—it should be remembered that the exercise of it, even when unavoidable, is always attended with a serious evil, namely, that the correction of legislative mistakes comes from the outside, and the people thus lose the political experience, and the moral education and stimulus that come from fighting the question out in the ordinary way, and correcting their own errors . . . The tendency of a

common and easy resort to this great function, now lamentably too common, is to dwarf the political capacity of the people, and to deaden its sense of moral responsibility.[24]

And this is the burden of Mr. Justice Frankfurter's argument in his opinion in the Gobitis case—an argument restated with masterly logic in his dissent in the more recent West Virginia flag salute case.[25] 'The precise issue,' he said in that earlier opinion,

> is whether the legislatures of the various states and the authorities in a thousand counties and school districts of this country are barred from determining the appropriateness of various means to evoke that unifying sentiment without which there can ultimately be no liberties . . . To stigmatize legislative judgment in providing for this universal gesture of respect for the symbol of our national life in the setting of the common school as a lawless inroad on that freedom of conscience which the Constitution protects, would amount to no less than a pronouncement of pedagogical and psychological dogma in a field where courts possess no marked and certainly no controlling competence . . . The wisdom of training children in patriotic impulses by those compulsions which necessarily pervade so much of the educational process is not for our independent judgment. Even were we convinced of the folly of such a measure, such belief would be no proof of its unconstitutionality. For ourselves, we might be tempted to say that the deepest patriotism is best engendered by giving unfettered scope to the most crotchety beliefs . . . But the court room is not the arena for debating issues of educational policy . . .

Judicial review itself a limitation on popular government, is a fundamental part of our constitutional scheme. But to the legislature no less than to courts is committed the guardianship of deeply cherished liberties. Where all the effective means of inducing political changes are left free from interference, education in the abandonment of foolish legislation is itself a training in liberty. To fight out the wise use of legislative authority in the forum of public opinion and before legislative assemblies rather than to transfer such a contest to the judicial arena, serves to vindicate the self-confidence of a free people.[26]

This is the crucial objection to judicial nullification of majority will in any field: that 'education in the abandonment of foolish legislation is itself a training in liberty.' If our democracy is less educated in this respect than we might wish, if our legislatures are less alert to constitutional principles than might seem desirable, a heavy responsibility rests upon the courts. For these, by taking over to themselves the peculiar guardianship of the Constitution and of civil liberties, have discouraged the people's active and intelligent interest in these matters. Judges—and liberals—have ignored what Professor Chafee finely says, that 'the victories of liberty of speech must be won in the mind before they are won in the courts.' [27]

For in the long run only an educated and enlightened democracy can hope to endure. Jefferson's faith in education is too familiar to justify rehearsal here, where he reared this splendid and imperishable monument to that faith.[28] But the implications of what is obvious are not always fully appreciated. For education, as Jefferson himself knew, is not just a matter of schooling. It is a continuous process, and education for effective participation in the business of democracy pretty much begins where formal schooling ends.

Here is one of the arresting differences between the democratic state and every other kind of state, that a democracy educates for continuous and active citizenship, whereas other forms of government educate only for passive obedience—and technical skills. The *sine qua non* of a successful democracy is that all citizens think for themselves about all issues that may arise; the requirement of successful totalitarianism is that citizens obey those who think for them.

This goes to the very heart of the problem of majority rule. 'That will to be right must be reasonable'—that is, it must appeal to reason. There can be no appeal to reason from the ultimate courts, not because there is no reason but because, in the nature of the institution, there is no appeal. The appeal must be, as Jefferson never wearied of pointing out, to the people. 'The mass of the people is the safest depository of their own rights.' [29] 'No government can continue good but under the control of the people.' [30] Or again, 'Above all things I hope the education of the common people will be attended to; convinced that on their good sense we may rely with the most security for the preservation of a due degree of liberty.' [31] 'Enlighten the people generally,' he wrote on another occasion, 'and tyranny and oppressions of body and mind will vanish like spirits at the dawn of day.' [32] And the first section of his proposed Bill for the More General Diffusion of Knowledge asserted that 'whereas . . . experience hath shewn, that even under the best forms, those entrusted with power have, in time . . . perverted it into tyranny; . . . it is believed that the most effectual means of preventing this would be, to illuminate, as far as practicable, the minds of the people at large, and more especially to give them knowledge of those facts, which history exhibiteth.' [33]

The people, in short, must be persuaded that any legislation which sets arbitrary limits to inquiry or discussion is treason to democracy not only—not even primarily—because it impairs minority rights, but because it denies to the majority itself that weapon without which democracy is paralyzed and impotent.

Liberalism has, indeed, emphasized overmuch the individual or minority interest in minority rights.[34] The interest is important and commands consideration. But even more important is the majority interest. It is easy enough to whip up sympathy for a Scopes, for the Scottsboro boys, for Kirk De Jonge, for the Gobitis children, but such sympathy is all too likely to be satisfied when some semblance of justice is done to the individual victim. The real task confronting us is to make clear to majorities that the interest of the whole of society is at stake in questions such as those raised by these hapless victims of legislation. The interest of all the people of Tennessee is at stake where legislation prevents the teaching of what is accepted elsewhere as scientific truth; the interest of all the people of Alabama —of the whole South, indeed—is at stake where it is possible to deny to anyone the accepted guarantees of a fair trial; the interest of the people of Oregon is at stake where participation in a public meeting to discuss public issues is a penal offense; the interest of all the children of Pennsylvania is at stake where mistaken methods are adopted to inculcate patriotism. It is a major educational task to persuade majorities of this, one which cannot be performed by the courts, which can and must be performed by the schools, the press, the church, political parties, and other democratic agencies. It is a task that has been neglected. I need not remind you of the consequences of that neglect today in Germany and Italy and the lesser nations that have felt the blight of totalitarian oppression. We are often reminded, by those who mistrust democracy, that the regimes of Hitler and of Mussolini and of lesser tyrants rest upon majority vote. They do not rest upon the vote of free majorities, of majorities educated to their responsibilities, of majorities sensitive to the interest of minorities and zealous to avail themselves of minority criticism.

I have attempted to present one of the crucial problems of American democracy—the problem of the 'conflicting claims of liberty and authority.' Ours is a government which rests squarely upon the consent of the governed, and which is designed to be controlled by the majority will. But ours is a government, too, which rests upon 'the laws of Nature and Nature's God,' and which is designed to protect certain inalienable rights from invasion even by the majority. To achieve the first objective Americans originated the great institution of the constitutional convention. To achieve the second they fashioned written constitutions and bills of rights. The purpose of these was not so much to prevent majorities from doing wrong in the realm of government as to prevent government from invading areas over which it had no jurisdiction whatever.

To conservatives, fearful especially for the sanctity of property, these guarantees were not sufficient. Zealous for the protection of minority rights, they formulated a philosophy of the 'tyranny of the majority' and took refuge in the denial of the majority will. They advanced, even, the curious argument that the United States was not a democracy but a republic and that the essence of republicanism was a balance of conflicting interests. Not content with limiting the jurisdiction of government, they were determined to limit the authority of government even where it had jurisdiction. To this end they added to the existing checks and balances the new institution of judicial review. And parallel with the development of majority rule throughout the nineteenth and twentieth century went the development and perfection of this technique for restraining majority rule.

The philosophical basis of judicial review is undemocratic. The purpose of judicial review is to restrain majorities. The assumption behind judicial review is that the people either do not understand the Constitution or will not respect it and that the courts do understand the Constitution and will respect it.

The assumptions and practices of the courts excited, as we have seen, the most passionate protests from Jefferson. He regarded judicial review as wrong in theory and dangerous in practice and prophesied that it would, in the end, imperil both democracy and the Union. He did not believe that judges were either better informed or more impartial than legislatures or executives. He was persuaded that the people were, in the long run, the safest depositories of all powers and that from errors of judgment on the part of their representatives the proper appeal was to the good sense of the mass.

An examination of the actual incidence of judicial review in the field of federal legislation would seem to support the Jeffersonian contention. It does not appear, from such an examination, that the courts are sounder in their interpretation of the Constitution or more tender of minority rights than are legislative bodies.

Nor is there any persuasive evidence from our own long and complex historical experience that majorities are given to contempt for constitutional limitations or for minority rights. Our majorities, state and federal alike, have been, to a remarkable extent, stable, law-abiding, and conservative. They have not justified any of the doleful jeremiads of Adams or Hamilton or their successors. They have not taxed wealth out of existence —there are and have long been more great fortunes here than elsewhere in the world; they have not crushed minorities; they have not set up dictatorships; they have not been hostile to education or to science. The pulpit, the press, the school, the forum, are as free here as anywhere else in the world—with the possible exception of that other great majority-rule country—Britain.

From the states, from time to time, there have been occasional departures from these high standards of constitutional integrity and, in the last quarter-century, the courts have intervened to protect victims of these lapses. From a short-range view this intervention has been desirable—it has saved individual victims and satisfied our desire that justice shall be done. From a longer perspective it may be doubted that judicial intervention has served a useful purpose. It has made for a confusion in our thinking about politics, it has supported the notion that what is constitutional is good, it has, above all, deprived democracy of its most effective training school —experience. It is relevant to recall that the framers of our Constitution carefully preserved the right to experiment. The grant of powers to the federal government was sufficiently broad—and general—to enable that government to adjust itself to the changing exigencies of a growing nation. And the only limitation put upon the states was the requirement that they shall have a 'republican' form of government—a term so vague it has never been satisfactorily interpreted and so broad as to permit almost any experiments within the democratic framework.

Our own experience, I believe, justifies Jefferson's faith that men need no masters—not even judges. It justifies us, too, in believing that majority will does not imperil minority rights, either in theory or in operation. It gives us firm basis for a belief that the people themselves can be trusted to realize that the majority has a vital interest in the preservation of an alert and critical minority and that, conversely, the minority can have no rights fundamentally inimical to the common wealth. It justifies us in the belief that only in a democracy where there is free play of ideas, where issues are freely fought out in the public forum,—where, in short, the safety valves of public discussion and experimentation and reconsideration are always open—can there be assurance that both majority and minority rights will be served. It is the glory of democracy that it—and it alone—can tolerate dissent. It is the strength of democracy that dissent, where tolerated, is helpful rather than harmful.

In a year when we turn back to Thomas Jefferson for inspiration and instruction in so many matters—and rarely in vain—we might do well to take more seriously his faith in majority rule and his fear of any institution which repudiates the philosophy of majority will or deprives it of the advantages of free play. We have less cause to fear the consequences of majority rule than had Jefferson, a century and a half ago. Only a democrat with limitless faith in the enduring strength of democracy could say—and it was proudly said:

If there be any among us who would wish to dissolve this Union or to change its republican form, let them stand undisturbed as monuments of the safety with which error of opinion may be tolerated where reason is left free to combat it.

We have no reason to be less confident of the ability of majorities to tolerate dissent or of the safety with which error may be tolerated where *reason* is left free to combat it.

NOTES

I

1. Minersville School District *v.* Gobitis, 310 U.S. 586. See also West Virginia State Board of Education *v.* Barnette, 63 S. Ct. Reporter 1178.
2. See references in 52 *Yale Law Journal* 175, n.
3. See F. J. Turner, 'Western State-making in the Revolutionary Era' in *The Significance of Sections in American History.*
4. These letters are reproduced in H. S. Commager, *Documents of American History*, no. 44.
5. See, for a penetrating analysis of the significance of this, A. C. McLaughlin, *The Foundations of American Constitutionalism*, ch. iv.
6. There is a thoughtful discussion of this in C. H. McIlwain, *Constitutionalism.*
7. See, for example, Jackson's veto of the recharter of the Second Bank of the United States: 'If the opinion of the Supreme Court covered the whole ground of this act, it ought not to control the coordinate authorities of the Government. The Congress, the Executive, and the Court must each for itself be guided by its own opinion of the Constitution . . . The opinion of the judges has no more authority over Congress than the opinion of Congress has over the judges, and on that point the President is independent of both. The authority of the Supreme Court must not, therefore, be permitted to control the Congress or the Executive when acting in their legislative capacities, but to have only such influence as the force of the reasoning may deserve.' Quoted in Commager, *Documents of American History*, no. 147.
8. *The Works of Abraham Lincoln*, II, 5.
9. George Pierson, *Tocqueville and Beaumont in America*, 726 ff.
10. A. de Tocqueville, *Democracy in America*, ed. John Bigelow, I, 271. See the whole of chapters 15 and 16 for Tocqueville's animadversions on the tyranny of the majority.

11. *The Works of John Adams,* ed. by Charles Francis Adams, VI, 7, 64, 9.
12. *The Works of Alexander Hamilton,* ed. by H. C. Lodge, I, 401.
13. N. H. Carter and W. L. Stone, *Reports of the Proceedings and Debates of the Convention of* 1821, pp. 219 ff.
14. See Rachel Luther *v.* Luther Borden and W. W. Story, *Life and Letters of Joseph Story,* II, 415.
15. See 'A Disquisition on Government,' in *Works* (Cralle ed.), I, *passim.*
16. See Webster's argument in the case of Luther *v.* Borden, *Works* (1851 ed.), VI, 217 ff.
17. See 'Reorganization of the Federal Judiciary,' U.S. 75th Cong. 1st Sess. *Sen. Comm. on the Judiciary, Hearings on,* 1392, 6 parts.
18. It is printed in *The Writings of Thomas Jefferson,* ed. by Paul Leicester Ford, II, 7 ff. (hereafter cited as Ford).
19. Ibid. III, 223.
20. 15 March 1789. Ibid. 223.
21. 4 Dec. 1790. *The Writings of Thomas Jefferson,* ed. by A. E. Lipscomb and A. E. Bergh, VII, 112 (hereafter cited as Memorial ed.)
22. 12 July 1816. Ibid. XV, 39.
23. 20 Dec. 1787. Ibid. VI, 392.
24. 16 Jan. 1787. Ibid. VI, 57.
25. 28 June 1804. Ibid. XI, 33.
26. 10 Dec. 1819. Ibid. XV, 234.
27. 6 Sept. 1819. Ibid. XV, 213-14.
28. 28 Sept. 1820. Ibid. XV, 278.
29. To Major John Cartwright, 5 June 1824. Ibid. XVI, 44-5.
30. 24 April 1816. Ibid. XIV, 489.
31. Ibid. XIV, 487.
32. See E. S. Corwin, 'The Constitution as Instrument and as Symbol,' 30 *Am. Pol. Sci. Rev.;* and Max Lerner, 'Constitution and Court as Symbols,' in *Ideas for the Ice Age,* pp. 232 ff.
33. See Luther *v.* Borden, 7 Howard 1 (1849); for a recent appreciation of the problem, Edwin Mims, Jr., *The Majority of the People.*
34. *The Right of the People to Establish Forms of Government.* Mr. Hallett's Argument in the Rhode Island Causes. Bost. 1848.
35. 12 July 1816. Memorial ed. XV, 41-2.

36. *Letters of LaFayette and Jefferson*, G. Chinard, ed., 80-81.
37. 6 Sept. 1789. Memorial ed. VII, 454 ff.
38. 24 June 1813. Ibid. XII, 270.
39. 16 July 1816. Ibid. XV, 46-7.
40. 24 Sept. 1823. Ibid. XV, 470.
41. See, for example, John Corbin, *Two Frontiers of Freedom*, and Isabel Paterson, *The God of the Machine*, ch. 12.
42. Jefferson himself usually used the word 'republican' rather than 'democrat' but it is reasonably clear that he thought they meant the same thing. See C. A. Beard, *Thomas Jefferson*. Address at the University of Virginia, 13 April 1943.
43. *The Anas*. 30 Dec. 1792. Memorial ed. I, 330.
44. 26 August 1816. Ibid. XV, 66.
45. 24 April 1816. Ibid. XIV, 490-91.
46. 12 July 1816. Ibid. XV, 33.
47. 28 May 1816. Ibid. XV, 19.
48. See H. S. Commager, 'Constitutional History and the Higher Law,' in Conyers Read, ed. *The Constitution Reconsidered*.
49. *The Federalist*, No. 78. But see no. 81 for some important qualifications of the principle here anounced.
50. 1 Cranch 137 (1803).

II

1. See Elliot's *Debates*, III, 152, 199, 200, 304, 314, 329; IV, 223. Letter to Madison, 6 Feb. 1788, Ford V, 5; to W. S. Smith, 2 Feb. 1788. Ibid. V, 2.
2. Kentucky Resolutions of 1798, Commager, *Documents* no. 102.
3. Kentucky Resolutions of 1799. Ibid. no. 103.
4. The constitutionality of the Alien and Sedition Acts did not come before the Supreme Court. The acts were sustained and applied, however, by judges in circuit courts. See F. M. Anderson, 'Enforcement of the Alien and Sedition Laws,' *American Historical Assoc. Reports*, 1912.
5. 22 July 1804. Memorial ed. XI, 42-3.
6. 9 March 1814. Ibid. XIV, 116.
7. Quoted in C. A. Beard, *Economic Origins of Jeffersonian Democracy*, 454-5.
8. July 1776. Memorial ed. IV, 258-9.
9. 11 Sept. 1804. Ibid. XI, 51.
10. To W. H. Torrance, 11 June 1815. Ibid. XIV, 304-5.

11. To John Breckinridge, 12 August 1803. Ibid. x, 410-11.
12. To Spencer Roane, 6 Sept. 1819. Ibid. xv, 213.
13. To Samuel Kercheval, 12 July 1816. Ibid. xv, 34.
14. Ibid. I, 120-22.
15. To Thomas Ritchie, 25 Dec. 1820. Ibid. xv, 298. See also letter to William T. Barry, 2 July 1822, ibid. xv, 388. 'We have erred in this point by copying England, where certainly it is a good thing to have the judges independent of the king. But we have omitted to copy their caution also, which makes a judge removable on the address of both legislative Houses. That there should be public functionaries independent of the nation, whatever may be their demerit, is a solecism in a republic of the first order of absurdity and inconsistency.'
16. 3 Feb. 1825. 'Early History of the University of Virginia . . .' in *Letters of Thomas Jefferson and Joseph C. Cabell*, 339.
17. 17 Feb. 1826. Memorial ed. XVI, 156.
18. On the influence of Story and the Harvard Law School, see Charles Warren, *History of the Harvard Law School*, chs. 23-5, 26, and Francis R. Aumann, *The Changing American Legal System*, chs. 5-7. It is interesting to note that within four years of Jefferson's death the law professor at the University of Virginia, John T. Lomax, was using Blackstone as a text. P. A. Bruce, *History of the University of Virginia*, II, 102.
19. The replies can be found in Elliot's *Debates*, IV, 533 ff.
20. Kent's *Commentaries* were published in 1826. See especially sections 448 ff.
21. Story's *Commentaries* were published in 1833. See especially sections 373 ff.
22. To Spencer Roane, 9 March 1821. Memorial ed. xv, 326.
23. To Thomas Ritchie, 25 Dec. 1820. Ibid. xv, 297.
24. To Charles Hammond, 18 Aug. 1821. Ibid. xv, 331.
25. To William B. Giles, 20 April 1807. Ibid. XI, 191.
26. To Edward Livingston, 25 March 1825. Ibid. XVI, 113.
27. To Caesar Rodney, 25 Sept. 1810. Ibid. XII, 425.
28. To Spencer Roane, 6 Sept. 1819. Ibid. xv, 213.
29. See John Taylor, *Construction Construed and Constitutions Vindicated*, and *New Views of the Constitution of the United States.*
30. See W. E. Dodd edition of Judge Roane's letters in the *John P. Branch Historical Papers*, 1904, 1905, and 1906; and W. E. Dodd, 'Chief Justice Marshall and Virginia,' *American Hist. Rev.* July

1907. It must be added that Taylor and Roane were not so much opposed to judicial review in principle as to the Supreme Court review of state court decisions. As Jefferson observed in a memorable letter to Roane, 'In denying the right they [the judges] usurp of exclusively explaining the Constitution, I go further than you do.' 6 Sept. 1819, Memorial ed. xv, 212-13.

31. G. C. Haines, *The American Doctrine of Judicial Review;* Louis Boudin, *Government by Judiciary* (2 vols.); E. S. Corwin, *The Twilight of the Supreme Court;* and Robert Jackson, *The Struggle for Judicial Supremacy* are the most penetrating of the many studies.
32. U.S. 75th Cong. 1st Sess. *Senate Comm. on Judiciary, Hearings on,* 1392, 6 parts. Here, too, Professor Haines and Mr. Jackson, who testified on behalf of the proposed bill, are exceptions to the generalization.
33. Quoted in 6 *Harvard Law Rev.* 33 n.
34. Marbury *v.* Madison, 1 Cranch 137.
35. Vegelahn *v.* Guntner, 167 Mass. 92.
36. The literature, pro and con, is large. See my article, 'Constitutional History and the Higher Law,' in Conyers Read, ed. *The Constitution Reconsidered;* R. Pound, 'Mechanical Jurisprudence,' 8 *Col. Law Rev.* 605; O. W. Holmes, 'The Path of the Law,' in *Collected Legal Papers;* Moses Aronson, 'Tendencies in American Jurisprudence,' 4 *Toronto Law J.* 90. For a criticism of 'realism,' see Kennedy, 'Storm over Law Schools,' 18 Thought 40.
37. To John Dickinson, 19 Dec. 1801. Memorial ed. x, 302.
38. To William Jarvis, 28 Sept. 1820. Ibid. xv, 277.
39. To Thomas Ritchie, 25 Dec. 1820. Ibid. xv, 298.
40. 'Autobiography.' Ibid. 1, 121.
41. Harlan in Standard Oil Co. of New Jersey *v.* U.S., 221 U.S. 1; Holmes in 'The Path of the Law,' *Collected Legal Papers,* 184; Stone in U.S. *v.* Butler, 297 U.S. 1.
42. For my summary of these cases I am indebted to H. W. Edgerton, 'The Incidence of Judicial Control over Congress,' 22 *Cornell Law Quart.,* 299.
43. It is extremely difficult to compile a list, but see Edgerton, op. cit.; C. Warren, *Congress, the Constitution, and the Supreme Court;* and *Provisions of Federal Law Held Unconstitutional by the Supreme Court,* published by the Library of Congress in 1936.

44. 1 Cranch 137.
45. 19 Howard 393.
46. It is not generally realized that Congress overrode this decision by Act of 19 June 1862 ending slavery in the Territories.
47. R. L. Mott, *Due Process of Law*, and E. S. Corwin, 'Doctrine of Due Process before the Civil War,' 24 *Harvard Law Rev.* 366 and 460.
48. 8 Wallace 603. Reversed in Legal Tender Cases, 12 Wallace 457.
49. 4 Wallace 333.
50. 13 Wallace 128.
51. 11 Wallace 113.
52. 253 U.S. 245.
53. 268 U.S. 501.
54. 92 U.S. 214.
55. 106 U.S. 629.
56. 109 U.S. 3.
57. 120 U.S. 678.
58. 190 U.S. 127.
59. 203 U.S. 1.
60. 230 U.S. 26.
61. 148 U.S. 312.
62. 158 U.S. 601.
63. 163 U.S. 228.
64. 208 U.S. 161.
65. 207 U.S. 463.
66. 213 U.S. 138.
67. 197 U.S. 488.
68. 256 U.S. 232.
69. 313 U.S. 299.
70. 247 U.S. 251.
71. 259 U.S. 20.
72. 252 U.S. 189.
73. 261 U.S. 525.
74. 255 U.S. 81.
75. Note, for example, the vague phrasing of the Sherman Anti-Trust Act: 'Every contract, combination in the form of trust *or otherwise*' (ital. mine)—language whose meaning, there is some ground to believe, was deliberately left for the courts to interpret. When the question of a tax upon the income of judges was before the House, the Chairman of the House Committee

said: 'I wish to say, that while there is considerable doubt as to the constitutionality of taxing . . . Federal judges' or the President's salaries . . . we cannot settle it; we have not the power to settle it. No power in the world can settle it except the Supreme Court of the United States. Let us raise it, as we have done, and let it be tested by . . : an appeal to the Supreme Court.' Quoted in Evans *v.* Gore, 253 U.S. 248 n. 1.

76. 259 U.S. 44.
77. 272 U.S. 52.
78. 295 U.S. 602.
79. 296 U.S. 287.
80. 297 U.S. 1.
81. 294 U.S. 330.
82. 295 U.S. 495.
83. Panama Refining Co. *v.* Ryan, 293 U.S. 389.
84. 295 U.S. 330.
85. 295 U.S. 555.
86. 298 U.S. 513.
87. 298 U.S. 238.

III

1. Quoted in Sean O'Faolin, *De Valera*, 115.
2. Carl Friedrich, *The New Belief in the Common Man.*
3. I am not forgetting Bacon's Rebellion, Shays' Rebellion, the Whiskey Rebellion, the Rent Wars, the fugitive-slave riots, the Dorr Rebellion, Vigilante activities in mining camps, the effective nullification of the Eighteenth Amendment, the Harlan County disturbances, or similar episodes that might be submitted. None of these was a 'revolution' or even a 'rebellion' in any proper meaning of the words. And I need not add that though secession and the war for Southern independence may have been rebellion, it was, in the view of those chiefly responsible for it, entirely legal and constitutional, and looked to the establishment of firmer constitutional guarantees than those which obtained in the Union.
4. Some Southerners would doubtless deny that their determination to maintain 'white supremacy' worked any real subversion of civil rights, or they would insist that the amendments were bad law, and ought not to be enforced or obeyed.
5. See J. T. Adams, *New England in the Republic*, ch. 6.

6. To Mr. Stiles, 24 Dec. 1786, Memorial ed. VI, 25.
7. 13 Nov. 1787. Ibid. VI, 372-3.
8. See letters to James Madison, 20 Dec. 1787, ibid. VI, 391; to T. B. Hollis, 2 July 1787, ibid. VI, 155-6; to David Hartley, 2 July 1787, ibid. VI, 151.
9. To John Adams, 28 Oct. 1813. Ibid. XIII, 397.
10. Lincoln Steffens, *Autobiography*, part 3, chs. 8, 19.
11. For these and other examples of legislative attack upon civil liberties, see Z. Chafee, *Free Speech in the United States*, pts. 2 and 3.
12. The citations are, seriatim: 299 U.S. 353; 268 U.S. 510; 273 U.S. 536; 274 U.S. 380; 283 U.S. 359; 310 U.S. 88; 301 U.S. 242; 309 U.S. 227; 287 U.S. 45; 283 U.S. 697; 307 U.S. 496; 303 U.S. 444.
13. See Chafee, op. cit. and Louis Lusky, 'Minority Rights and the Public Interest,' 52 *Yale Law J.* 1.
14. 304 U.S. 144 at 152 n. 4.
15. To David Hartley, 2 July 1787. Memorial ed. VI, 151.
16. Grosjean *v.* American Press Co. 297 U.S. 233.
17. Lovell *v.* Griffin, 303 U.S. 444; Jamison *v.* State of Texas, 63 S. Ct. Reporter 669.
18. Tileston *v.* Ullman, 63 S. Ct. Reporter, 493.
19. Minersville School District *v.* Gobitis, 310 U.S. 586 and West Virginia State Board of Education *v.* Barnette, 63 S. Ct. Reporter 1178.
20. *In re* Jacobs, 98 N.Y. 98.
21. Ritchie *v.* People, 40 N.E. 454. See also People *v.* Williams, 189 N.Y. 131.
22. Law and Politics, 197.
23. L. Lusky, op. cit. 2.
24. J. B. Thayer, John Marshall, 106.
25. 63 S. Ct. Reporter, 1178.
26. 310 U.S. 586.
27. *Free Speech in the United States*, 325.
28. These lectures were given at the University of Virginia.
29. To John Taylor, 28 May 1816, Memorial ed. XV, 23.
30. To John Adams, 10 Dec. 1819, Ford ed. X, 153.
31. To James Madison, 20 Dec. 1784, Ford ed. IV, 480.
32. To Du Pont de Nemours, 24 April 1816, Ford ed. X, 25.
33. Ford ed. II, 221-2.
34. See Lusky, op. cit.

Made in the USA
Middletown, DE
15 June 2023

32672638R00059